Emily

Emily™/MD

A new musical based on
Emily of New Moon, Emily Climbs
and *Emily's Quest*
by L.M. Montgomery

BOOK AND LYRICS
Richard Ouzounian
&
MUSIC
Marek Norman

McArthur & Company
Toronto

Canadian Cataloguing in Publication Data

Ouzounian, Richard, 1950-
Emily

Based on Emily climbs, Emily of New Moon and Emily's quest by L.M. Montgomery. Includes music for 4 songs.
ISBN 1-55278-139-9

I. Norman, Marek. II. Montgomery, L.M. (Lucy Maud), 1874-1942. Emily climbs. III. Montgomery, L.M. (Lucy Maud), 1874-1942. Emily of New Moon. IV. Montgomery, L.M. (Lucy Maud), 1874-1942. Emily's quest. V. Title.

PS8579.U96E45 2000 C812'.54 C00-930296-4
PR9199.3.096E45 2000

Composition, Design and Cover by *Michael P. Callaghan*
Typeset at *Moons of Jupiter, Inc.* (Toronto)
Printed in Canada by *Transcontinental Printing Inc.*

McArthur & Company
322 King Street West, Suite 402
Toronto, ON, M5V 1J2

10 9 8 7 6 5 4 3 2 1

The publisher wishes to acknowledge the financial support of the Government of Canada through the Book Publishing Industry Development Program (BPIDP) for our publishing activities.

This is dedicated to my children,
Katherine and Michael:

I promise stars above,
to guide your way.
You'll find a world of love,
and see it stay.
What you've been dreaming of
is yours one day.
I promise you
it all comes true…

June 2000, Toronto

NOTES ON *EMILY*

"This is where the dream begins . . . "

For me, the dream of writing a musical based on work by Lucy Maud Montgomery began thirty years before the event took place. Until I was nineteen years old, I had never heard of Lucy Maud Montgomery. Please forgive me. I was born in New York City, and this great Canadian writer's works were not part of the normal cultural kit of the average American teenage boy.

However, the summer of 1969 found me on my first trip to London. And on the first Friday night in June, I had no particular plans. I found myself outside the New Theater, looking up at the marquee of a show called *Anne of Green Gables*. I hadn't heard of anyone connected with it, except for the leading lady Polly James, who had stolen my heart in *Half a Sixpence* a few years before on Broadway. But the critical quotes were glowing, including one from Harold Hobson from the Sunday *Times* that said, "This was an evening when it was good to be alive and in a theater."

That settled it. I bought a ticket, went inside, and for the next two and a half hours, I laughed, cried and enjoyed myself thoroughly. If you had told me that over the next quarter-century I would get to know and work with many of the people who had shaped that evening, I would have pronounced you crazy. But indeed, that's what happened. And the wonderful Norman and Elaine Campbell, Don Harron, Susan Anderson, as well as the now-sadly-missed Barbara Hamilton and Alan Lund became my professional colleagues over the years.

But what of the lady whose work began it all? Well, I wish I could tell you that I rushed right out and purchased the original book by Lucy Maud Montgomery, but that took four more years.

Let's leap ahead to 1973. By now I had moved to Canada, worked on my M.A. at the University of British Columbia, and started a professional directing career. For a variety of reasons, I found myself flying to Prince Edward Island to visit the Charlottetown Festival. I soon put two and two together, and realized this is where that amazing musical *Anne of Green Gables* had been created and was still filling the theater at every performance. I saw the show again, loved it again, and this time, I bought a copy of the novel that had inspired it.

It was a revelation. I had been expecting a "girl's book" of the simplest and most sentimental sort. Instead, I was greeted with a work full of dry wit, profound feeling and absolutely beautiful writing. I was hooked.

While still visiting the Festival, I purchased the next books in the series, *Anne of Avonlea* and *Anne of the Island*. And a dream took shape in my head. I wanted to write a musical based on a book by Lucy Maud Montgomery.

At first I thought it would have to be a sequel to *Anne,* and that's the fantasy I clung to for years. The year 1992 found me (along with my collaborator Marek Norman) writing a musical for the Charlottetown Festival called *The Great Adventure.*

Once again, the combined magic of the Island, the Festival and Lucy Maud cast its spell on me, and I actually began writing *Anne of Avonlea*, as I planned to call it. Jacques LeMay, who was artistic director at the time, liked the idea, but there were far too many problems involving copyrights and clearances, and we let the whole thing move to the back burner.

Five years later, on a beautiful August night, I found myself sitting outside the stage door of the Confederation Centre in Charlottetown having dinner with Curtis Barlow, the new gentleman in charge of the Festival. Just before dessert, he asked the question I had been waiting for: would Marek and I consider writing a musical for the Festival? Would we? You bet, and we even had the idea. I started to tell him about *Anne of Avonlea*, but he shook his head. No, he didn't want a sequel to *Anne of Green Gables*, but he *did* want a musical based on a book by Lucy Maud Montgomery. Had I ever read *Emily of New Moon*?

I hadn't, but I vowed to get a copy as soon as I could. I don't think Curtis anticipated how quickly I would. The next morning, I was on the first flight to Toronto, with a brief stopover in Halifax. I knew there was a bookstore at the airport, and I prayed for two things: that it would be open, and that it would have a copy of *Emily of New Moon*.

God was smiling (as He often did on this project), and I dashed back on to the plane, with a copy of *Emily* that would become my closest companion for the next little while. Within five minutes, it was obvious that this book would make a wonderful musical. Some of my very first lyrics came directly from the novel: "The house in the hollow was a mile from anywhere, the lonesomest place in the world." As soon as

I landed in Toronto, I phoned Marek, and told him to get a copy of our next project.

My original enthusiasm was tempered by one thing. As I finished the book, I realized that although in many ways it was *different* from *Anne of Green Gables*, there were many ways in which it was the same: orphan girls on Prince Edward Island having trouble with stern female guardians and vixenish schoolmates and finding consolation in bosom chums and sweet older men.

Without telling Curtis or Marek, I went ahead and read the other two books of the trilogy: *Emily Climbs* and *Emily's Quest*. As I read, my enthusiasm grew and grew. Taken as a whole, these three books told the story of Emily and her growth as a woman and an artist. This was something exciting, especially after a conversation I had with the novelist Carol Shields. This wonderful and generous author is a huge fan of Lucy Maud Montgomery, both as a writer of fiction and non-fiction.

It was Carol who urged me to read the Montgomery journals, which I did, and it was around this time, after having closely examined the texture and pattern of Montgomery's life, that I suddenly came upon the key to how *Emily* would have to be written:

Emily Starr's life turned out the way that Lucy Maud Montgomery wished hers had.

Emily stayed on the Island; Lucy Maud left. Emily waited to marry a kindred spirit; Lucy Maud didn't. Emily devoted her life to her art; Lucy Maud had to squeeze her writing in around duties at the Parsonage.

Once I realized all of this, the actual writing of the musical fairly flew. Of course, there were problems compressing three novels into one evening. Fans of the books may find one or more of their favorite passages missing, but I hope they'll always find the intent to be true. I actually only allowed myself one major piece of rewriting. The character of Mr. Carpenter, Emily's benefactor and teacher, was combined with Dean Priest, Emily's cousin and suitor. A certain amount of contemporary squeamishness made me eliminate the consanguinity and have Dean first encounter Emily when she was a bit older and safely out of Lolita country.

EMILY was first performed by Marek and me in the spring of 1998 for an audience of three: our wives and Curtis Barlow. All three of them approved (most notably Curtis!) and we went ahead with a workshop that August.

From that performance we learned that the show had a powerful emotional pull on an audience, and we needed to mold and shape it a bit more. That we did over the fall and winter, and it finally went into rehearsal in spring of 1999 under the loving direction of Jackie Maxwell.

Jackie brought so much to that first production, as did choreographer Valerie Moore, designers Sue LePage and Rob Thomson, orchestrator Jim Pirie, conductor Fen Watkin, and my dear friend and collaborator, musical director Marek Norman.

I also can't speak of that marvelous first experience without thanking each and every one of the cast who brought Lucy Maud Montgomery's creations to vivid theatrical life. The tremendous response of the audience on opening night will remain one of the happiest memories of my career. When Tracy Michalidis stepped forward after her bow as Emily and started to lead the cast in singing "This Island" the whole theater seemed united in one wave of pure emotion.

Why do I love this island?
Why do I love this land?
There's something in its beauty
that I understand.

The copper of its beaches,
and the silver of its shore.
It is these,
and so much more.

I know I love this island,
this place that stands apart.
I welcome every morning
as it fills my heart.

I know I love its people,
and I know that they are strong,
and I know
that I belong.

I believe the hand of God will guide me
as I live between the sea and sky.
And I pray my children stand beside me
for it's here I'll stay until I die.

I wished that Lucy Maud Montgomery had been there to hear it, and I felt that I was beginning to repay the debt for the evening of magic that *Anne of Green Gables* had given me thirty years before.

Like they say: what goes around, comes around.

— RICHARD OUZOUNIAN

THE FIRST PERFORMANCE OF EMILY TOOK PLACE AT THE CONFEDERATION CENTRE FOR THE ARTS IN CHARLOTTETOWN, PRINCE EDWARD ISLAND, ON JUNE 19, 1999.

The cast: (in alphabetical order)

Graham Coffeng (Ensemble)
Sarah Daurie (Ensemble)
Raquel Duffy (Ilse)
Denise Fergusson (Aunt Elizabeth)
Kerry Gage (Ensemble)
Paul Guitard (Ensemble)
Marlene Handrahan (Miss Brownell)
David Hughes (Ensemble)
Mary Kelly (Mrs. McIntyre)
Glenda Landry (Mrs. Bradshaw)
Cliff LeJeune (Dean Priest)
Jeff Madden (Teddy)
Stephanie Manchulenko (Ensemble)
Elizabeth Mawson (Ensemble)
David McMullen (Ensemble)
Tracy Michalidis (Emily)
Julain Molnar (Aunt Laura)
Mike Nadajewski (Perry)
Declan O'Reilly (Douglas Starr/Dr. Burnley)
Craig Ramsay (Ensemble)
Lisa Rubin (Ensemble)
Sharmaine Ryan (Jennie Strang)
Hank Stinson (Cousin Jimmy)
Kelly Straughan (Ensemble)
Mari Trainor (Janet Royal)
Jeff Wong (Ensemble)

Stage Manager: **Jane Butler**
Assistant Stage Managers: **Judy Joe, Larry Copeland**

Director and Dramaturge: **Jackie Maxwell**
Musical Director: **Marek Norman**
Choreographer: **Valerie Moore**
Set and Costume Designer: **Sue LePage**
Lighting Designer: **Robert Thomson**
Orchestrator: **Jim Pirie**
Conductor: **Fen Watkin**
Associate to the Musical Director: **Neil Bartram**

Executive Director and CEO of the
Confederation Centre: **Curtis Barlow**

Tracy Michailidis as Emily,
The Charlottetown Festival, 1999 PHOTO BY BARRETT & MACKAY

ACT I

I

(The lights fade and the curtain rises to reveal a large empty space, illuminated only by a clear night sky. A young girl with dark hair appears, carrying a small book and gazing intently at the space around her. This is EMILY. She begins to write in the book. As she does so, we hear wind chimes, and the COMPANY gradually appear around her.)

EMILY:

I see a star,
I see it shine now
I see it shine through the night,
to the day.
It lights the path
that will be mine now,
come what might,
come what may.
I see the sky
so dark and steady.
I see the moon,
how it grins.
The heavens smile
and I am ready.
For this is where
the dream begins.

(As the ENSEMBLE sing, the empty space gradually transforms to the location that they are describing.)

Ensemble:

Oh, the house in the hollow
was a mile from anywhere,
the lonesomest place in the world.
It grew up in the hollow
like a big, brown mushroom that
was hidden away from the world.

There's a long green lane
with a circle of birches,
where the light never looks,
where the sun never searches.

And the thin, dry grass
that has barely been tended
shows the way to a door
that is rarely befriended.

But the house in the hollow
that may seem so bleak
has a glow you can find from afar:
it's the love of Douglas and Emily Starr.

(Inside the house, lying on a settee, wrapped in a shawl is DOUGLAS STARR. He is a man in his forties, obviously once very handsome, but now frail and near death from consumption.)

Douglas:

Emily, do you remember your mother?

Emily:

Just a little here and there . . . like lovely bits of dreams.

(The vision of JULIET appears: young and beautiful, pale and shimmering.)

DOUGLAS:

Juliet . . . Juliet Murray . . . she was one of the Murrays that live up on the North Shore at New Moon Farm . . . folks up there call them "the chosen people."

(The ENSEMBLE gradually turn into the dark-coated MURRAYS they sing of.)

VOICE #1:

The Murrays are an old lot,
they came here years ago.

VOICE #2:

The Murrays are a cold lot,
there isn't much they show.

VOICE #3:

The Murrays take their feelings
and lock them up inside.

ALL THREE:

Then they throw away the key,
and the only thing you see
is the Murray pride.

DOUGLAS:

The old stock at New Moon is pretty well run out. Only your Aunts Elizabeth and Laura live there now, and your Cousin Jimmy. They never married. "Couldn't find anyone good enough for a Murray," it used to be said.

Ensemble:

The Murrays are an old lot,
they came here years ago.
The Murrays are a cold lot,
there isn't much they show . . .

Douglas:

I was a writer with nothing in the world but his pen and his ambition, and when your mother married me, her family would have nothing more to do with her.

(The MURRAYS shun JULIET, and she vanishes into the darkness.)

Ensemble:

The Murrays take their feelings
and lock them up inside.

Ensemble & Douglas

Then they throw away the key,
and the only thing you see

Douglas:

is the Murray pride.

Douglas:

And yet she was never sorry for marrying me.

Emily:

Of course she wouldn't be sorry! She'd rather have you than all the Murrays of any kind of a moon.

DOUGLAS:

We were so happy, Emily. And you were the child of that happiness.

Emily just beginning,
Emily one day old.
Life is a lovely story,
wait till you hear it told.

Emily in my arms now,
Emily sound asleep.
I will make you a promise,
one that I vow to keep.

I promise stars above,
to guide your way.
You'll find a world of love,
and see it stay.
What you've been dreaming of
is yours one day.
I promise you, I promise you,
it all comes true.

Welcome, my darling daughter,
Emily Murray Starr.
None of us know where life will lead.
How can I give you all you'll need?
How could I guess the joy you'd bring so far?
Dearest Emily, Emily,
oh, what a gift you are!

I'll be with your mother again, very soon.

EMILY:
I wish you could take me with you.

DOUGLAS:
No, you must stay. But first, you must learn to find words for your thoughts, your feelings. Oh, Emily . . . you will love deeply and you will suffer terribly, for that is the path you have chosen . . . may God be with you.

EMILY: *(embracing him)*
I love you, Father.

DOUGLAS:
Dearest Emily, Emily, Emily,
how can I say goodbye?

(DOUGLAS disappears into the shadows as the ENSEMBLE transform the setting into a funeral, with STARR's coffin surrounded by MOURNERS.)

ENSEMBLE:
Oh, the house in the hollow
was a mile from anywhere,
the lonesomest place in the world.

MINISTER:
Dearest Lord, please receive here the poor soul of your servant. Let us pray for the late Douglas Starr.

ENSEMBLE:
Let us pray for the late Douglas Starr.

EMILY:
No . . . Father . . .

(EMILY kneels and places the book on the ground, near the coffin.)

MINISTER:
Your father is with God, Emily . . . this is your family now.

(The MURRAYS all draw lots during the following:)

MURRAY #1:
I don't know who she looks like.

MURRAY #2:
She's not a Murray . . . that's plain to see.

MURRAY #3:
She's not much to look at.

MURRAY #4:
She's got her father's forehead.

MURRAY #5:
She's got her mother's eyes.

MURRAY #6:
No, Juliet was much prettier than that . . . *(A general babble of discussion as they begin to compare their lots.)*

EMILY:
Stop discussing me as if I weren't here! You have no right to talk about me at all!

(Silence as a grim woman with a great air of command holds up the short straw. This is AUNT ELIZABETH.)

MINISTER:
It looks like you've got your work cut out for you, Elizabeth.

ELIZABETH:
Indeed.

EMILY:
What do you mean?

MINISTER:
This is your Aunt Elizabeth. You're to stay with her at New Moon.

(A strange, almost elfin man breaks through the crowd, dragging a shy, retiring woman: COUSIN JIMMY and AUNT LAURA.)

JIMMY:
With *us*. I'm your Cousin Jimmy, and this is your Aunt Laura.

EMILY: *(to MINISTER)*
Am I to have no say in the matter?

ELIZABETH:
There is no choice. Your father left you without a cent . . . what a miserable failure!

EMILY:
Father wasn't a failure! Nobody who was loved as much as he was could ever be a failure . . .

ELIZABETH: *(long pause)*
We will leave for New Moon in five minutes, and Emily, you will come with us.

(They all exit, except for JIMMY, who notices the book on the ground and lags behind to give it to EMILY.)

JIMMY:
Emily, Emily . . .

EMILY:
Cousin Jimmy?

JIMMY:
I have something for you . . . something you forgot. Here. *(He hands her the book.)*

EMILY: *(without enthusiasm)*
Thank you, but I don't feel like writing any more. Not without Father.

JIMMY:
You may not feel like it now, but you will. You'll find words for your thoughts, for your feelings.

EMILY:
That's just what Father said! But how will I know what I should write?

JIMMY:
Oh don't worry, you will . . . now say your good-byes to this place.

(JIMMY exits.)

EMILY:

I will, but I have to take one last look at the trees, and the clouds, and the sky. It seems like they're calling to me. They're saying: "You will never forget this place. It will live in your heart forever." (*She opens the book and writes:*) "You will never forget this place. It will live in your heart forever. "

(The music swells, and the lights build around EMILY, as the night sky vanishes, and the day begins to dawn around her.)

ENSEMBLE: *(returning)*

Oh, the dream begins,
and the dreamer stands here glowing,
finally knowing
how and why.
Yes, the dream begins,
but there's no more fear of failing,
she is sailing
through the sky,
through the sky!

EMILY:

I feel the breeze,
I feel it blowing
I feel it blow from the sea
to the shore.
It shows the way
my life is going,
ever free,
ever more.
I feel the sun
in all its glory.

I feel the earth,
how it spins.
I was born
to tell this story.

Yes, I was born
to tell this story.
this is how
this is when
this is where the dream begins!

(Everything swirls around EMILY as the day comes to life around her. ELIZABETH, LAURA and JIMMY enter with her trunk and lead her off. The music continues as she sees all the PEOPLE of the Island as she starts her journey. We finally arrive at New Moon, and we are outside the house.)

JIMMY: *(pointing to an attic window)*
Look up there, Emily . . . that's where you'll stay.

LAURA:
It was your mother's room . . .

EMILY:
Way up there?

JIMMY:
At the top of the steepest flight of stairs on the North Shore. Almost halfway to heaven.

EMILY:
Then I'll be closer to Father.

ELIZABETH:
Will you listen to her? Head in the clouds . . . must be the Starr in her. Just like her father.

EMILY:
Indeed, Aunt Elizabeth, I *am* just like my father.

JIMMY: *(to LAURA)*
See those flaming eyes . . . I think she's just like Douglas.

LAURA:
But she has Juliet's dreamy smile.

ELIZABETH:
Nonsense! No Murray was ever a dreamer.

JIMMY:
I'm a dreamer, and proud of it.

ELIZABETH:
Aye, you've got moonbeams in your head, James Murray.

JIMMY:
And who put them there, Elizabeth?

LAURA:
Not in front of the child.

EMILY:
Why do you keep discussing me as if I weren't here!

ELIZABETH:
Because you're a child, and not a person!

EMILY:
I am very much a person, Aunt Elizabeth.

JIMMY:
Emily . . .

ELIZABETH:
Jimmy, Laura, you take the bags inside. I'll bring her back to Earth . . . *(They exit, EMILY is looking up at her room.)* Emily, what are you staring at nothing in that queer way for?

EMILY:
I wasn't staring at nothing.

ELIZABETH:
Don't do it again. It gives your face an unnatural expression.

EMILY:
It's the only expression I have, Aunt Elizabeth.

ELIZABETH:
I don't want any of your pertness, Miss. You have said quite enough!

EMILY:
If I feel something, then I must let it come out.

Elizabeth: *(trying to hold her temper)*
We have a saying here: "Was there ever easier work than keeping the mouth shut?" That's the Murray way. *(LAURA has re-entered and listens, unseen.)*

Emily:
Fine. Then I will keep my mouth shut and put all thoughts into my poetry.

Elizabeth:
Poetry? Learn one thing, young lady: there is no poetry allowed in this house.

Laura: *(to diffuse the situation)*
Elizabeth, don't you think Emily would enjoy a walk in the orchard?

Elizabeth:
That's a fine idea, young lady. Start you thinking about apples instead of poems.

Emily:
Aunt Elizabeth, it is my destiny to be a poet, and I will follow that destiny. A Starr must be true . . .

Elizabeth:
And a Murray must be stubborn. *(To LAURA)* Heaven help us all!

(ELIZABETH and LAURA exit into the house. EMILY wanders around outside and finally crosses to a large leafy tree, makes herself comfortable on the ground, and writes:)

EMILY:

"Now Autumn comes ripe
  with the peach and the pear,
The sportsman's horn is heard
  throughout the land . . . "

(We hear a young man's VOICE from deep in the branches of the tree.)

VOICE:
There's no peaches on the Island, girl, and I never heard a sportsman's horn neither.

EMILY:
Come down from that tree at once . . . whoever you are.

(A cheeky but appealing young man named PERRY sticks his head through the branches and smiles at EMILY.)

PERRY:
I guess you don't have to stick too close to facts in poetry.

EMILY:
What do you know about poetry?

PERRY:
Enough to know that yours don't rhyme.

EMILY:
It's blank verse.

PERRY:
Very blank.

EMILY:
I don't know if we should be speaking. We haven't been properly introduced.

PERRY:
Oh, I know who you are . . .

EMILY:
You do?

PERRY:
You're Miss Emily Starr, the orphan niece.

EMILY:
And who are you?

PERRY:
I'm the chore boy at New Moon . . . name's Perry Miller. I live over to Stovepipe Town.

EMILY:
Stovepipe Town?

PERRY:
We're so poor there the houses got no chimneys, only pipes stickin' out of the roof.

EMILY:
I don't believe you.

PERRY:
Then come up here and see for yourself.

EMILY:
Polite young ladies do not climb trees.

PERRY:
Then what's stopping *you*?

EMILY:
Of all the impertinent, ill-mannered . . .

PERRY:
Up you go. *(PERRY extends a hand, and helps EMILY up the tree.)*

EMILY: *(looking around)*
Oh . . . oh! It's so beautiful up here! I must write it down.

(EMILY is too enraptured to notice, but PERRY sees LAURA enter from the house and looks up at them in the tree. Some TOWNSPEOPLE have gathered as well.)

PERRY:
You don't have time for poetry now.

EMILY:
Why not?

PERRY:
Because Miss Laura has spotted us.

EMILY:
You'd better help me back to the ground.

PERRY:
I can't. There's only one way down.

EMILY: *(trying to be composed)*
And what way might that be?

PERRY:
Jump.

(EMILY looks down and emits a lady-like little scream.)

LAURA: *(hearing the scream)*
Jimmy, it's Emily, she's caught up in a tree!

JIMMY:
Don't do anything, Emily, we're coming to get you!

(JIMMY and the TOWNSPEOPLE get a ladder and help EMILY down.)

LAURA:
Are you all right, dear? Say something.

(PERRY suddenly reappears, having snuck down the back of the tree in all the confusion.)

PERRY:
How about something in blank verse?

EMILY:
Why, you double-dealing, double-crossing, good-for-nothing . . .

(ELIZABETH enters from the house.)

ELIZABETH:
What is the meaning of this?

PERRY:
It's all my fault, Miz Murray, I told Emily to climb the tree.

ELIZABETH:
The more fool her for listening to you.

LAURA: *(crossing to EMILY)*
Are you all right, dear?

ELIZABETH:
The child is fine, Laura, no thanks to her own willfulness.

EMILY:
That's not fair.

ELIZABETH:
Life is not fair, Emily. If it were, I would not be compelled to take care of you. Don't you all have chores to do? Surely today hasn't changed to the Sabbath when my back was turned?

JIMMY: *(sotto voce)*
It wouldn't dare.

(PERRY, JIMMY, LAURA and the TOWNSPEOPLE exit. ELIZABETH thrusts a horrid striped sunbonnet and apron at EMILY.)

ELIZABETH:
Here, put on this apron and sunbonnet.

EMILY:
They're frightful!

ELIZABETH:
They were your mother's when she was a little girl.

EMILY: *(struggling into apron)*
Then no wonder she ran away with Father.

ELIZABETH:
You're just like your mother, self-willed and stubborn and determined to ruin your life! Well, I won't have it. Not a second time.

(ELIZABETH and EMILY glare at each other as the scene changes around them to the schoolyard with CHILDREN playing, skipping, happily making noise, etc. until the bell rings and a seemingly sweet but starchy teacher named MISS BROWNELL appears.)

MISS BROWNELL:
Good morning, Miss Murray . . . and this must be Emily.

ELIZABETH:
You'll find her difficult, Miss Brownell, I certainly do. But you're the one to drum some sense into her, if anyone can.

MISS BROWNELL:
I'm sure Emily and I will become good friends.

ELIZABETH:
That would certainly be interesting to see. Good luck, Miss Brownell. Good day, Emily. Please be a credit to the family. That's the Murray way. *(ELIZABETH exits.)*

MISS BROWNELL:
Well, Emily, I'm sure you will be happy here at Blair Water School.

EMILY:
Indeed, Miss Brownell? I wish I shared your certainty.

MISS BROWNELL: *(in a new and chillier tone)*
We'll have none of your Murray pride here, young lady.

EMILY:
I'm not a Murray!

MISS BROWNELL:
Don't put on any airs with me. I think it's time you learned your place around here.

(A vicious little pig-tailed vixen named JENNIE STRANG pops to the front.)

JENNIE:
At the bottom of the heap.

MISS BROWNELL:
Emily, this is Jennie Strang,. If you work hard, one day you might be as bright and pretty and popular as she is . . .

JENNIE:
Ha! *(JENNIE pushes EMILY's sunbonnet down to cover her face. The others all laugh.)*

MISS BROWNELL:
. . . but somehow, I doubt it. Jennie, introduce Emily to the rest of the class. They've been so looking forward to seeing the new Murray girl. *(MISS BROWNELL withdraws.)*

EMILY:
I told you, I'm not a Murray!

JENNIE:
Oh, yes you are!

GIRL #2:
Look at those buttoned boots!

GIRL #3:
And that ridiculous apron.

GIRL #4:
Will you look at that sunbonnet?

GIRL #5:
For her complexion!

Girl #6:
That's the Murray pride!

Girls:
The Murrays are an old lot,
they came here years ago.
The Murrays are a cold lot,
there isn't much they show.
The Murrays take their feelings
and lock them up inside.
Then they throw away the key,
and the only thing you see
is the Murray pride,
the Murray pride, the Murray pride, the . . .

Emily:
Stop it, all of you! You have no right to talk about me like that!

Miss Brownell:
Why are you so vain and haughty?
What gives you that lofty air?

Jennie:
Acting like the Queen of Sheba,
when you're just a prickly pear.

Miss Brownell:
Dressed up in your boots and bonnet,
puffed up like a popinjay.

Jennie:
You'll be getting your comeuppance,
come the final Judgment Day.

Girls:

We know the Bible tells us
about the sin of Pride.
Worst of the Seven Deadly,
the evil you can't hide.

And so prepare, you sinner,
to hear that trumpet call.
Because it's pride, pride, pride, pride, pride
that goes before the fall.

Boy #1:

What do the Murrays have to be so proud about, anyway?

Girl #3:

Your Aunts are both old maids.

Boy #2:

And your Cousin Jimmy is an idiot.

Emily:

He has more sense than any of you!

Miss Brownell:

Yes, Emily, but what is *your* special gift?

Boys and Girls:

Can you cook?
Can you sew?
Can you dance?
Can you sing?

JENNIE:

Can you knit?

BOY #1:

Or crochet?

GIRLS, BOYS and MISS BROWNELL:

Can you do . . . . . . anything?

EMILY:

I can!

BOYS and GIRLS:

Says you!
So what, exactly, can you do?

EMILY:

I can write poetry.

JENNIE:

You lie!

EMILY:

A Starr does not lie.

BOY #3:

Then let's hear some of your poetry.

EMILY:

Never.

JENNIE:

I bet it's in that little book she carries . . .

Boy #4:
Then let's get it!

Emily:
No!

(A dance sequence ensues, with the BOYS and GIRLS trying to grab EMILY's book away from her.)

Boys and Girls:
And so prepare, you sinner,
to hear that trumpet call.
Because it's pride, pride, pride, pride, pride
that goes before the . . .

(EMILY does indeed fall, and they snatch the book and bring it to JENNIE.)

Jennie:
And now, let's read some of her precious poetry.

(She is interrupted by the sudden Valkyrie-like entrance of ILSE BURNLEY, a strange but appealing girl, dressed in a mismatched assortment of clothes.)

Ilse:
Give me that book, Jennie Strang.

Jennie:
This isn't any of your business, Ilse Burnley.

Ilse:
Oh, isn't it? Don't sass me, piggy-eyes. Give me the book.

Boy #5: *(snatching the book and holding it aloft)*
Then come and get it, Ilse.

(ILSE takes the offensive this time, pursuing all the other boys and girls.)

Boys and Girls:
And so prepare, you sinner,
to hear that trumpet call.
Because it's pride . . .

Girls:
Pride . . .

Boys:
Pride . . .

Girls:
Pride . . .

All: *(except EMILY & ILSE)*
Pride, pride, pride, pride, pride,
that goes before the . . .

Ilse:
. . . fall!

(ILSE grabs the book and sends them all crashing down.)

All:
Goes before the fall!

Emily: *(as ILSE hands her the book)*
Why, thank you.

ILSE:
Ilse. Ilse Burnley. Think nothing of it. They're jealous of you, that's all. Look here, Emily Starr, I want you for my chum. You can tell me things. And I can tell you things. I haven't anybody to tell things to.

EMILY: *(a bit hesitant)*
If you want me to.

ILSE:
Nobody likes me, you know. Not even my father. But they'll be sorry when I grow up.

EMILY:
Why?

ILSE:
Because I am going to be a world-famous actress. Don't laugh. I will! What about you?

EMILY:
I'm going to be a poet.

ILSE:
Can you really write poetry?

EMILY:
Here, judge for yourself . . .

(ILSE takes the book and starts to scan it rapidly.)

ILSE:
Emily Starr, did you make all these poems up out of your own head?

EMILY:
I did.

ILSE:
Well, then, I guess you *are* a poet, all right. *(She calls out.)* Oh, Miss Brownell!

EMILY:
What are you doing?

ILSE:
I want the whole class to hear what a great poet you are.

EMILY:
Those poems are private, Ilse.

ILSE:
Don't be silly. If they're so private, then why did you write them down? Miss Brownell . . .

EMILY: *(turning to ice)*
That book is my personal property, and you will give it back to me at once!

ILSE:
Well! You little puling, sniveling chit, you're never going to boss me around like that again.

EMILY:
You're absolutely right. Because I'm not going to associate with you ever again.

ILSE:
I'm glad to be rid of you, you proud, stuck-up, conceited, top-lofty *biped*!

MISS BROWNELL:
What's the problem, Ilse?

ILSE:
If I couldn't write better poetry than you, Emily Starr, I'd hang myself.

EMILY:
I'd lend you a dime to buy the rope.

ILSE:
You go to the devil!

(ILSE storms off. EMILY starts to follow her, but is stopped by MISS BROWNELL.)

MISS BROWNELL:
Just a minute, Emily, I think we'd all like to see what's in this book that's caused so much trouble. *(She begins to read it.)*

EMILY:
Please, please, Miss Brownell, please don't read it! It isn't anything!

MISS BROWNELL:
You are too modest, Emily. It is a book of *poetry*. And I am sure we would all enjoy this *poetry*. Am I right, children?

Boys and Girls:
Yes, Miss Brownell.

Miss Brownell: *(reading)*
"Lilies lifted up white cups
For the bees to dr-r-i-i-nk." *(BOYS and GIRLS laugh.)*

Emily: *(snatches her book back)*
I didn't write it that way!

Miss Brownell:
Give me the book, Emily.

Emily:
These poems are mine. You have no right to them. You are an unjust, tyrannical person!

Miss Brownell:
Indeed? Then we shall see what your Aunt Elizabeth has to say about this.

Jennie:
School's out!

(And as MISS BROWNELL and EMILY glare at each other, the schoolyard vanishes and we are back in the kitchen at New Moon.)

Emily:
Please, Aunt Elizabeth.

Elizabeth:
Not another word! I have heard the whole story. Kneel down here before Miss Brownell and ask her pardon for your conduct today.

Emily:
Aunt Elizabeth, please let me tell my side of the story!

Elizabeth:
You will do as I say, or you will be an outcast in this house. No one will have anything to do with you until you have obeyed me. Now kneel.

Jimmy:
A human being should not kneel to any one but God.

Laura:
He's right, Elizabeth.

Elizabeth: *(a pause, then)*
Indeed. But you must apologize to your teacher.

Emily: *(turns to face MISS BROWNELL)*
If I did anything wrong today, I ask your pardon for it.

Miss Brownell: *(with a wry smile)*
My, my, you have the most original way of apologizing here in the Murray household. Good day to all of you. *(She exits.)*

Elizabeth:
I will take that book of poetry from you now.

Emily:
No, you cannot do that to me!

ELIZABETH:
It is time you learned who is mistress here, young lady.

EMILY:
No, the book is mine. *(EMILY speaks in a strangely commanding voice.)* Let me hear no more of that.

ELIZABETH:
What . . . what did you say?

EMILY:
Let me hear no more of that.

LAURA:
What is the matter, Elizabeth?

ELIZABETH:
I saw Father . . . looking from her face. And she said "Let me hear no more of that" just as he always said it. His very words.

EMILY: *(puzzled)*
Aunt Elizabeth?

ELIZABETH:
All right, Emily, you may keep your book. But you are not to waste any more time in writing poetry, do you understand? No more poetry . . . *(ELIZABETH exits.)*

EMILY:
Aunt Laura, I don't understand.

LAURA:
I must get supper on the table.

EMILY:
Please, Aunt Laura, tell me.

LAURA:
Elizabeth was sitting here, reading a book of poems that a young man had given to her. Father came in, saw his supper wasn't ready, and threw the book into the fire, saying "Let me hear no more of that." And from that day on, this house has known no poetry, or love or laughter . . . until now.

(LAURA exits. EMILY moves over to the corner where JIMMY has been sitting, silently whittling all during this.)

EMILY:
Cousin Jimmy, what am I supposed to do? If I can't write poetry, then what *can* I write?

JIMMY:
Well, you can write letters, to friends you left behind.

EMILY:
I didn't have any friends but Father. (*An idea dawns.)* Father! Oh, Cousin Jimmy, thank you so much!

JIMMY:
For what, child?

EMILY:

For the gift of inspiration! *(EMILY races up to her room.)*

JIMMY:

Be careful on those stairs, Emily! *(He shakes his head and exits.)*

(We are in EMILY's attic room.)

EMILY:

I must write to Father and tell him everything. *(She opens her book and begins:)* "To Mr. Douglas Starr, On the Road to Heaven. Oh Father, what a day full of events this has been! I have found my first enemy, Jennie Strang, and my first friend, Ilse Burnley. Only I'm not so sure she's still my friend, because we had a fight . . . "

(ILSE enters, dragging a battered steamer trunk, and we are in another space, ILSE's house, on the next day.)

ILSE:

Oh piddle and tosh, I've forgotten all about that.

EMILY:

But you got so angry with me in the schoolyard?

ILSE:

Well, now I'm glad you're here.

(DR. BURNLEY enters. He is a handsome man with a brusque manner.)

Dr. Burnley:
Ilse, I'm off to deliver the Bradshaw baby at Malvern Point. If I'm not home, find yourself something to eat and try to get to sleep before dawn. *(He spots EMILY.)* Good day . . . whoever you are. *(He has gone.)*

Emily:
Is your father always like that?

Ilse:
No.

Emily:
Thank goodness.

Ilse:
This was one of his cheerier days. Everyone says he's like that because of my mother.

Emily:
What happened to her, Ilse?

Ilse:
I don't know exactly. She went away when I was a baby. That's all my father would tell me, so I stopped asking. I don't care about the real world anyway. I live in here. *(She indicates a battered steamer trunk she's been sitting on.)*

Emily:
What is that?

ILSE:

It's what every great actress needs: a trunk to hold her memories. *(ILSE starts hurling assorted odds and ends around.)* The parts she's played, the cities she's seen, the lovers she's betrayed.

EMILY:

Have you betrayed many lovers?

ILSE:

Not yet, but I'm working on it. *(She puts a large jeweled headpiece on.)* This was from my Titania. Did you see it? Pity. *(She flings some lurid drapery over her shoulder.)* And this was from my Helen of Troy. Father says it makes me look positively Euripidean. I don't know what that means, but it sounds awfully good. Oh Emily, believe me, this is the only life to lead!

Powder and paint,
satin and lace,
rouge on my cheek,
smile on my face.
That's how you're gonna see me.
Top of the bill,
slaying them all.
Toast of the town,
belle of the ball.
They're gonna "joie de vie" me.

Out there in the limelight,
the time might
say I'm right
to play a part on the stage where I was
born to be.

EMILY:

That's fine for you, Ilse! An actress is supposed to be glamorous. But I'm going to be a distinguished poet, and a poet has to be . . .

ILSE:

Dull.

EMILY:

Thoughtful.

ILSE:

Thoughtful is no fun, Emily. You just follow me.

ILSE (and EMILY):

Paper and pen, (paper and pen)
that's how it starts. (that's how it starts)
One little verse,
hundreds of hearts. (hundreds of hearts)

ILSE:

We'll give 'em grand finales.

BOTH:

Batting our eyes
tossing our curls . . .

EMILY:

Sipping champagne.

ILSE:

Swingin' my pearls.

BOTH:
We'll play the femmes fatalleys!

EMILY and ILSE:
The actress and poet
both know it,
and show it,
for we belong to a life that's fine
and fancy free.

ILSE:
We'll be the rage

EMILY:
of every age

ILSE:
both on the stage

EMILY:
and on the page.

BOTH:
We'll light up the sky for all eternity!

(TEDDY KENT comes upon the girls, in all of their "finery". He is a shy, gentle, attractive young man, carrying a sketch pad.)

TEDDY:
Well, Miss Burnley, I see the theatrical spirit hasn't left you.

ILSE:
Master Kent, what are you doing here?

TEDDY:
It was getting boring just sitting at home so I thought I'd pay you a visit. *(He spots EMILY.)* I'm Teddy Kent.

EMILY:
Emily Starr. I haven't seen you at school.

ILSE:
Teddy's been ill.

TEDDY: *(looking at EMILY)*
But I'm feeling much better now. *(TEDDY holds out his sketch pad.)* Here, Emily. *(ILSE clears her throat.)* . . . and Ilse . . . I wanted you to see some of my drawings.

EMILY: *(takes them first)*
Teddy, they're wonderful!

ILSE:
He's one of us, Emily.

TEDDY: *(smiling at EMILY)*
What does she mean?

EMILY: *(blushing)*
Let Ilse tell you.

ILSE:
We're all dreamers, Mr. Kent, dreaming of rainbow gold. You're an artist, Emily's a poet, and I *(dramatic pose)* am an actress.

TEDDY:
Gosh, I'd never have guessed!

ILSE:
Powder and paint

TEDDY:
Color and light

EMILY:
Paper and pen

ALL THREE:
Getting it right.
we're gonna make them hear us.

Gonna be great
gonna be grand
see it appear
here in my hand.
The world is gonna cheer us.

(TEDDY shows the girls the countryside in front of them.)

TEDDY:
Do you see those three paths? I call the first one the Yesterday Road, because it used to be lovely,

but it isn't any more. And that one in the middle is the Today Road, because it is lovely right now. But that one over there, well, it may not look like much at the moment, but I promise you it *is* going to be lovely someday. That's the Tomorrow Road, my friends, and that's the road we're all on.

ALL THREE:
We'll be the rage
of every age,
both on the stage,
and on the page.
we'll light up the sky for all eternity!

Get what you want,
be what you ain't.
All that you need
is powder and paint.
Powder and paint!

(The three of them run off as the TOWNSPEOPLE change the scene around them, filling in the seasonal activity of life on the Island.)

TOWNSPEOPLE:
Springtime is for sowing,
summer is for growing.
Autumn is for reaping,
winter is for keeping.

Start at the beginning,
see the seasons spinning.
Funny, how they go so fast!
Look, another year has past.

(We come on ELIZABETH and LAURA hanging laundry, while JIMMY trots along, holding the basket.)

ELIZABETH:
A petticoat? With a blue ribbon? You spoil her, Laura.

LAURA:
It's the child's birthday. It's only right we mark the occasion.

JIMMY:
What bothers you more, Elizabeth? The petticoat or the ribbon?

ELIZABETH:
A child doesn't need to be spoiled with presents.

JIMMY:
Then who bought her that brand-new dictionary?

ELIZABETH:
Look at how high that sun is, and I haven't started the midday meal.

JIMMY:
Elizabeth . . .

ELIZABETH:
We're not going to stop her from writing all those words, so she might as well learn to spell them properly. That's the Murray way. *(She exits.)*

JIMMY: *(with a twinkle)*
That's the Murray way. *(He exits.)*

LAURA: *(wryly)*
That's the Murray Way. *(She exits.)*

(CHILDREN run across the stage on their way to the beach. EMILY enters last, writing in her book.)

EMILY:
"Dear Father, I am fourteen years old today. I wrote a letter 'from myself at fourteen to myself at twenty-four,' sealed it up and put it away to be opened on my twenty-fourth birthday. I only hope Aunt Elizabeth doesn't read it. She's *such* a Murray, proud and cold, and empty deep inside."

PERRY:
Come on, Emily, we're all going down to the beach.

EMILY:
Not just now, Perry, thank you very much. *(She starts to turn away.)*

PERRY:
You don't fancy me, do you? I see it in the kind of smile you give me. All prim and proper. Not like the smiles you give Teddy Kent, the kind he puts in all his pictures.

EMILY:
He does nothing of the sort!

PERRY:
It doesn't bother me. You see, when I grow up, I mean to ask you to marry me. Oh, I know what you think: I'm nothing but Stovepipe Town. But

one day, I'm going to be the prime minister of Canada.

Emily:
Indeed, Mr. Miller?

Perry:
Indeed, Miss Starr. *(Neither of them see ILSE creeping up behind them.)* I know Ilse's the one who's crazy about me, but I don't know if I could put up with her.

Ilse:
Put up with *me*? You conceited homo sapiens! I wouldn't put up with *you* if my very life, my soul, my being, my essential existence depended upon it!

(ILSE storms off.)

Perry:
I didn't know she liked me *that* much!

(PERRY follows her off. EMILY, laughing, tags along. The TOWNSPEOPLE change the scene to autumn.)

Townspeople:
Try and you'll keep learning,
watch it all returning.
See the way the seasons fly.
Look, another year's gone by.

(It is evening. JIMMY is sitting by a large boiling cauldron. EMILY, TEDDY, PERRY and ILSE are at his feet.)

JIMMY:
This is how you know another year has passed and the autumn has truly come, not by the changing of the leaves, or the harvesting of the crops, but by old Jimmy Murray boiling the pigs' potatoes.

TEDDY:
Seems like a lot of work to me.

JIMMY:
It's one of my jobs.

EMILY:
Like tending the garden.

JIMMY:
Just so, Emily. Elizabeth bosses the farm, but she leaves me some places of my own to make up for . . . *(He stops.)*

EMILY:
For what, Cousin Jimmy?

JIMMY: *(a pause, then)*
We were just children, and we were playing tag around the well. I made Elizabeth mad, and she went to give me a bang on the head. I stepped back to get out of the way, and down I went. My head struck the stones at the side. I was took up for dead. *(He shakes his head.)* I got about after a while, though, pretty near as good as new . . . Even though some folks say I've never been quite right ever since.

PERRY:
Those folks don't know anything.

JIMMY:
Oh, I see things, Master Perry, that's how I knew Emily was a poet.

TEDDY:
And what are we, Jimmy?

JIMMY:
You're all blessed children, and you shall be whatever it is you dream of being.

ILSE:
I like the sound of that!

JIMMY:
But you, Emily, you have something more. The gift, the second sight, I see it in you. Your great-grandmother was a Highland woman and they say she had it. Now it passes on to you

EMILY:
What do you mean?

JIMMY:
Three times in your life you will see things that are past all mortal ken . . . and with what you see, you will save three people: the first, your dearest friend, the next, a total stranger, and the last, your own true love.

Emily:
How will I know, Cousin Jimmy?

Jimmy:
You just will, Emily . . . that's the wonderful thing about the world: we finally know all the things we were meant to know. Believe me.

(The scene changes to the winter, and the center of the stage is a frozen rink, with some TOWNSPEOPLE watching, some skating.)

Women:
Celebrate the seasons,
add up all the reasons.

Men:
Why we love this life is clear.

Women:
Look . . .

All:
Here comes another year.

Ilse:
How wonderful! You finally joined the human race and got a pair of skates!

Emily:
Aunt Laura bought them for me, but Aunt Elizabeth won't let me use them.

Dr. Burnley:
Why isn't Emily skating?

Elizabeth:
Too much cold air isn't good for her health. Her father died of consumption.

Dr. Burnley:
Indeed, that's why she ought to be outside all the time . . . Emily, out on the ice, I'll show you how it's done! *(He skates off with EMILY. ILSE, left behind, follows them.)*

Laura:
Allan is awfully kind to Emily.

Elizabeth:
He's not so kind to his own flesh and blood. It almost seems as though he still blames Ilse for everything that her mother did.

Laura:
Sometimes it's easier to blame than to forgive.

Elizabeth:
Forget about him, Laura. The man will never marry again.

Emily:
What man will never marry again? Dr. Burnley?

Elizabeth:
There are some things young ears were not meant to hear.

EMILY:
My ears are sixteen years old, just like the rest of me.

ELIZABETH:
Don't be pert, young lady . . . and don't stay out too long, whatever Dr. Burnley says. Are you coming, Laura?

LAURA:
In a bit.

ELIZABETH:
First ice of the season and all of Blair Water goes crazy . . . I've never understood it, and I never will.

(ELIZABETH exits, and the skating continues. DR. BURNLEY offers his arm to LAURA, PERRY winds up with ILSE, and TEDDY with EMILY.)

TOWNSPEOPLE:
Springtime is for sowing,
summer is for growing.
Autumn is for reaping,
winter is for keeping.
Celebrate the seasons,
add up all the reasons:
why we love this life is clear.
Look, here comes another year!

(Everyone departs, two by two, leaving EMILY and TEDDY alone.)

TEDDY:
I'm glad we could be by ourselves for a little while.

EMILY:
Teddy, where are we going?

TEDDY:
A special place of mine . . . a place I've wanted you to see for a long time. *(They arrive at a clearing with the shell of a small house that has never been finished.)* Here it is.

EMILY:
What happened to it, Teddy?

TEDDY:
A man named Fred Clifford began to build it for his fiancée, but when it was this far along, she jilted him . . . and that was the end of it.

EMILY:
Do you ever wonder what it would have been like if they'd finished it?

TEDDY:
All the time.

EMILY:
I'd put two comfy chairs by the fire, bookcases against that wall. It could be wonderful!

TEDDY:
And every night, on my way home, I'd whistle to let you know I was coming. *(He demonstrates an odd little whistle.)*

EMILY:
And I'd be waiting for you at the door.

TEDDY:
I knew you'd love it. That's why I brought you here.

EMILY:
Poor old place. It looks . . . disappointed.

TEDDY:
That's just the word.

Disappointed house,
sitting all alone,
dreaming of a love
it has never known.

Out there in the yard
no one climbs the tree.
All the doors are locked,
no one has the key.

No one climbs the stair,
no one dims the light.
When it's dark and cold,
no one holds you tight.

Dreaming of a love,
it has never known.
Disappointed house,
sitting all alone.

But imagine
if the two of us were there,
just imagine
all the happiness we'd share.
Days so splendid
that you wish they'll never end.
But they do,
and then you
will look up to find a friend.

We'll awaken
to the morning God has made.
Toast and bacon,
and a pot of marmalade.
I'll sit painting,
and you'll write the whole day through.
You and me,
sipping tea,
while our dreams are coming true.

EMILY:
It's very late. We . . . we'd better be going.

TEDDY:
But we'll come back again, won't we?

EMILY:
Yes, we will. It looks different now.

TEDDY:
It *is* different now.

(As he sings, they walk back home, and the setting changes to New Moon.)

Disappointed house,
let the love begin.
Throw the shutters wide,
show the sunlight in.

We have found the key,
open up the door.
For the disappointed house
won't be disappointed any more.

(TEDDY is about to kiss her.)

LAURA'S VOICE:
Emily, is that you?

EMILY:
Yes, Aunt Laura.

LAURA'S VOICE:
Say good night to Teddy . . . it's very late.

EMILY: *(mock solemnity, shaking his hand)*
Good night, Teddy.

BOTH: *(they break into giggles)*
It's very late!

(TEDDY dashes off, laughing, and EMILY crosses into the kitchen.)

LAURA:
I was wondering where you were.

EMILY:
Teddy and I had the most magical evening.

LAURA:
I'm happy for you, child.

EMILY:
You seemed to be having a wonderful time skating with Dr. Burnley.

LAURA:
He's a very nice man.

EMILY:
I think you find him more than just "very nice."

LAURA:
I have no idea what you mean.

EMILY:
I'm sure you have every idea, and that's why you're blushing like a sunset.

LAURA:
You're too young to know these things.

EMILY:
I'm old enough to know about you and Dr. Burnley.

LAURA:

Allan . . . Most people thought we were intended.
They say he had bought me a diamond necklace.
But then he met her . . . Beatrice Mitchell.

(We see a vision of the glamorous BEATRICE MITCHELL, holding up a glittering diamond necklace.)

He gave her the necklace. And his heart . . .

Oh, she was beautiful,
and she was delicate.
Yes, she was everything a woman wants to be.
When Allan walked with her,
and she would smile at him,
he looked at her the way he never looked
at me.

She had a tiny mark,
right there above her brow,
and when I think of it, that's when the
memory starts.
That little heart-shaped flaw
made Allan love her more.
He used to tell us all she was the ace
of hearts.

The ace of hearts
had won the king.
She had his child,
she wore his ring.
The queen's true love
had disappeared.
The stage was set:
the knave appeared.

He was a handsome man
who roamed the seven seas,
and he had loved our lady many years ago.
He sailed into her life,
and when he smiled at her
she thought of all the passion that they used
  to know.

His touch was magical,
his arms were welcoming,
and then he whispered that at midnight
  he departs.
So on that moonless night,
the lady slipped from sight,
and that's the last we ever saw the ace
of hearts.

The ace of hearts
betrayed the king.
Gave up her child,
lost everything.
She'll love the knave
eternally.
They share a grave
beneath the sea.

And when he heard the news,
then Allan lost his heart.
They say it's buried with his bride beneath
  the sea.
Poor Ilse lives alone,
without a father's love,
and what I felt for him is just a memory.

Now he's a widower,
I am a maiden aunt,
and when the curtain's up, we all must play
our parts.
No matter what you feel,
you take the hand they deal,
for you can never win against the ace of hearts,
for you can never win against the ace of hearts.

EMILY:
Oh, Aunt Laura . . .

(EMILY kneels at LAURA's feet and embraces her.)

LAURA: *(stroking her brow)*
There, there. Emily, you feel so warm . . . are you all right?

(ELIZABETH suddenly appears, clutching EMILY's book.)

ELIZABETH:
She is not all right! She is a deceitful child who has been writing the most hateful things, writing them to her Father, if you please! So, Emily, you think that I am *(reading)* "proud and cold, and empty deep inside?"

EMILY: (*snatching it away from her.)*
How dare you? How dare you read my private papers?

ELIZABETH:
You were a penniless orphan, and I took you into my home. I have given you food and shelter and kindness, and now *this* is my thanks!

EMILY:
You had no business to read my letters to Father.

ELIZABETH:
They are disgraceful, and must be destroyed!

EMILY:
No! I'd sooner burn myself. You shall not have them. Let me hear no more of that.

ELIZABETH:
Keep your letters, and scorn the old woman who opened her home to you. I need no love from the likes of you. I need no love from anyone!

(EMILY suddenly faints at ELIZABETH's feet.)

LAURA:
Dear child!

ELIZABETH:
What is it?

LAURA:
She's burning up with fever.

ELIZABETH:
I don't know. Jimmy, fetch Dr. Burnley, and hurry!

(They make a bed for EMILY. Time passes. DR. BURNLEY enters.)

ELIZABETH:
Tell me plainly, Allan, is there any danger?

DR. BURNLEY:
She's had this fever for five days now.

LAURA:
And she's hysterical. She keeps babbling some nonsense about a missing woman and an open well.

ELIZABETH:
What can we do, Allan?

DR. BURNLEY:
You're a God-fearing woman, aren't you, Elizabeth? Then pray to Him now. Pray for your Emily. *(DR. BURNLEY exits.)*

ELIZABETH:
Oh Laura, is this all my fault?

LAURA:
Calm yourself, Elizabeth.

ELIZABETH:
If the child doesn't get better . . .

(ELIZABETH can't finish the sentence. EMILY stirs in her fever dream.)

EMILY:
The well in Mr. Lee's field is open. Someone will fall into it. Why doesn't Mr. Lee cover it up?

LAURA:
What do you mean, dear?

EMILY:
I see her coming over the fields. She is coming so gladly, she is thinking of her Baby . . . she doesn't see the well. It's so dark, she doesn't see it . . . she doesn't see it. No!

ELIZABETH:
What is wrong?

EMILY:
I saw her.

ELIZABETH: *(calmly)*
Who did you see? Who did you see, Emily?

EMILY:
The Ace of Hearts . . . Ilse's mother . . . she didn't run away. She fell into the old well. She's there now. Go and get her out. Promise me.

ELIZABETH:
Yes, I'll get her out if she is in there.

EMILY:
I know you'll keep your word. You are very hard, but you never lie, Aunt Elizabeth. You never lie.

ELIZABETH:
Jimmy, go over to Thomas Lee's and ask him to come here.

LAURA:
Elizabeth, you don't really mean to have that old well searched?

Elizabeth:
I do indeed. I'll keep my word to the child.

(JIMMY exits. The lights fade, time passes, EMILY sleeps. JIMMY re-enters, and without a word, hands the diamond necklace to LAURA.)

Dr. Burnley: *(entering a beat later)*
How is Emily?

Elizabeth:
The fever's gone down.

Dr. Burnley:
I'll go see her.

Laura:
No.

Dr. Burnley:
What's wrong?

Elizabeth:
Oh Allan, may Beatrice forgive us for what we thought all these years . . . and may Ilse forgive you now.

Dr. Burnley: *(to LAURA)*
Beatrice? Ilse? What are you talking about? What did you find?

(LAURA hands DR. BURNLEY the necklace, touches his cheek. He crosses outside .)

JIMMY:
. . . with what she sees, she will save three people: the first, her dearest friend . . .

LAURA:
No matter what you feel,
you take the hand they deal,
for you can never win against the ace of hearts.

(The scene changes to the school at Blair Water. The school day is ending, and PERRY is supervising the decorations for a party.)

ILSE:
Well, Mr. Miller, I see you're going to great heights to get things ready for the party.

PERRY:
I thought Emily was coming back to school today.

ILSE:
Maybe she wasn't quite ready yet.

PERRY:
Gosh sakes, Ilse, she's been gone the whole term.

ILSE:
Gosh sakes, Perry, someone might think you missed her.

PERRY:
Well, I do.

ILSE:
I'll remember that when you ask me to dance tonight.

PERRY:
Who said I was going to ask you?

ILSE:
Don't worry . . . you will.

(ILSE exits. PERRY shouts after her.)

PERRY:
Well, maybe I won't! *(He softens.)* And maybe I will.

(PERRY exits. EMILY enters, and TEDDY, who has been waiting, runs up to her.)

TEDDY:
Emily! I began to think you weren't coming.

EMILY:
It's the last day at Blair Water School . . . I couldn't miss that.

TEDDY:
All those years we spent here, finally done. And now, a new world begins.

EMILY:
Ilse will train to be a famous actress.

TEDDY:
Perry will learn how to run the country.

EMILY:
You will become the finest artist the world has ever seen.

TEDDY:
And you, the greatest poet.

EMILY:
Only if I can find the way, Teddy.

TEDDY:
The way?

EMILY:
The way to turn the feelings of my heart into the words of my pen.

TEDDY:
But Emily, you've done that already.

EMILY:
No, I haven't. Not really.

TEDDY:
I gave your poems to the new teacher, just like you told me to, and he wants to meet you to talk about them.

EMILY:
Mr. Priest? What's he like, Teddy?

TEDDY:
He's very smart but mind you, he's a bit strange. Maybe it's because of how he looks. One arm is

withered, and one shoulder is higher than the other. That's why we call him Jarback.

(DEAN PRIEST has entered. Tall, dark, forbidding, with one shoulder higher than the other, just as TEDDY has described.)

PRIEST: *(overlapping with TEDDY)*
Jarback . . . Jarback Priest . . . I'm only crippled, Mr. Kent, not deaf and blind.

TEDDY:
Mr. Priest, I . . .

PRIEST:
Good day, Kent. You must be the legendary Emily Starr. Yes, Starr is the proper name for you . . . I said good day, Kent.

EMILY:
Thank you, Teddy . . . I'll be fine. *(TEDDY exits, reluctantly.)*

PRIEST:
Shall we stay outside, Starr? The light of late afternoon is perfect for discussing poetry, don't you think?

EMILY:
If you say so, Mr. Priest.

PRIEST:
So demure! Where is that famous Starr spirit I've heard so much about?

EMILY:

When I have a reason to show it, sir, you will surely see it.

PRIEST:

Let us begin with your poems. *(PRIEST begins leafing through her poems.)* "Life, as thy gift, I ask no rainbow joy." . . . Is that true, girl?

EMILY:

No. I do want rainbow joy. Lots of it.

PRIEST:

We all do. But very few of us get it. And this: "With the chilly calm on her brow/That only the dead may wear." Have you ever seen the chilly calm on the brow of the dead?

EMILY:

Yes I have. When I buried my father, six years ago.

PRIEST:

You must have loved him very much.

EMILY:

Have you nothing more to say of my poetry?

PRIEST:

What is there to say? A few good lines out of hundreds. That's not enough. I know you *want* to be a writer, Starr, but . . .

(EMILY blocks out his words as she walks away.)

EMILY:

Oh, the dream begins,
but the dreamer stands here waiting,
hesitating,
wondering why.
Yes, the dream begins,
but the dreamer fears she'll fail now.
Will she sail now
through the sky?

(PRIEST has been leafing through her book, reading her letters.)

PRIEST:

Starr, why didn't you show me these first?

EMILY:

Those are letters to my father, they shouldn't be in there!

PRIEST:

But they are brilliant writing, girl.

EMILY:

That isn't writing! That is what I feel, and hope, and dream . . .

PRIEST:

That's what writing *should* be, Starr. You have the gift, child. But you don't know the steep ascent ahead of you. You will stay in the valley if you're wise.

EMILY:
I cannot! I must climb the Alpine Path, and write my name on the scroll of fame.

PRIEST: *(laughing)*
Where did you ever get such a literary notion?

EMILY:
From a poem I read.

PRIEST:
From a poem you read! From this day forward, Starr . . . all your notions must come from your heart . . . not from other people's poems. And if they do . . .

I promise stars above,
to guide your way.

(The spirit of DOUGLAS STARR appears and continues with him:)

DOUGLAS and PRIEST:
You'll find a world of love,
and see it stay.
What you've been dreaming of
is yours one day.
I promise you
it all comes true.

DOUGLAS:
You will love deeply and you will suffer terribly, for that is the path you have chosen. May God be with you.

EMILY:
Thank you, Father, thank you.

(She holds her letters and poems up, and the ENSEMBLE take them away, like leaves being carried by the wind.

PERRY and TEDDY enter from opposite sides of the stage, and the four men look on EMILY as they sing.)

PRIEST, TEDDY, PERRY, DOUGLAS:
Aching to find tomorrow,
making each moment last.
This is the way the world moves on,
blink of an eye, the girl is gone.
Suddenly, there's a woman whirling past.
Tell me, Emily, Emily,
how did you grow so fast?

(The four of them vanish, leaving EMILY alone on the beach, silhouetted against a glowing sunset.)

EMILY:
Here I stand
at seventeen,
so many things
I haven't seen.

So much to do,
so much to try.
I'll touch the earth,
I'll reach the sky.

Set me free,
let me be
where the dawn is breaking.
For I know
I must go
where a world of wonder is mine for the
taking.

Here and now,
I'll make a vow
to say what's in my heart
while I'm waiting for the world
to start.

(PERRY, ILSE and TEDDY enter, all dressed for the celebration.)

PERRY:
Here I stand
at seventeen,
fresh as grass.

ILSE:
And twice as green.

PERRY:
So many hopes,
so many fears.

ILSE:
And still so wet
behind the ears.

TEDDY:

Take me where
I can share
all that God is giving.
Me and you,
bright and new,
for the day is dawning and life is for living.

EMILY, TEDDY, PERRY and ILSE:

Four in one
who've just begun
to learn that life's an art,
while we're waiting for the world
to start.

(The TOWNSPEOPLE all enter, and the dance begins. A highlight is a newly cheerful DR. BURNLEY dancing with ILSE.

As the dance reaches its climax, everyone stands on the beach to greet the sunrise.)

ALL:

Seventeen,
and unafraid
to face a world
we (they) never made.
We (they) don't ask why,
we (they) don't ask how.
We (they) want it all,
we (they) want it now.

EMILY, TEDDY, ILSE, and PERRY:

Let today
light the way

to a new beginning,
Every eye
aiming high . . .

ALL:

For the race we're (they're) running is well
worth the winning.

EMILY:

Here and now,
I'll make a vow
to say what's in my heart.

ALL:

While we're (they're) waiting for the world
waiting for the world.
waiting for the world,
waiting for the world, for the world
to start!

(The curtain falls on the whole COMPANY, with EMILY, TEDDY, ILSE and PERRY up front, waiting to face the future.)

(End of ACT I)

ACT II

II
Four Years Later.

(The entr'acte features a ballet that takes our young people on a journey of four years. It ends with them all assembling prior to leaving Blair Water to pursue their various dreams. PERRY is going to be the first to leave, but at the last minute he discovers he's lost his train ticket. He dashes off in pursuit of it, and returns just in time.)

ALL:
Twenty-one,
the waiting's done,
we'd (they'd) best be on our (their) way.
Cause we're (they're) ready for the world
today.

(The departure begins behind ILSE and EMILY.)

ILSE:
Emily, it's our last summer together.

EMILY:
I don't want to think about it.

ILSE:
You have to. Perry leaves today, if he can ever find his ticket, and Teddy and I sail for England in September.

EMILY:
All chasing after rainbow gold: the lawyer, the artist and the actress.

ILSE:
But what about the writer?

EMILY:
She's stuck, Ilse, like a wheel in a rut, going round and round, not going anywhere.

ILSE:
Oh, but you will! You'll be a great writer, Emily, I know it. All you need is something to write about.

(Two Island women, MRS. BRADSHAW and MRS. HOLLINGER, enter in great distress.)

MRS. BRADSHAW:
Ilse, Ilse . . .

ILSE:
Mrs. Bradshaw, what's wrong?

MRS. BRADSHAW:
You haven't seen my little boy, have you? My Billy?

ILSE:
No, we haven't.

EMILY:
What happened to him?

Mrs. Hollinger:
He went missing after dinner three nights ago.

Mrs. Bradshaw:
Where can he be? Where can my boy be?

Mrs. Hollinger:
Calm yourself, Clara. we'll find him.

Mrs. Bradshaw:
No we won't! He's dead, I tell you, I know he's dead.

Emily:
He isn't dead. *(EMILY seems to slip into a trance-like state.)* I see a boy. He has red hair . . .

Mrs. Bradshaw:
That's my Billy! Where is he?

Ilse:
Emily?

Emily:
He's in the Disappointed House.

Mrs. Hollinger:
Where?

Ilse:
The old Clifford place.

Mrs. Hollinger:
We looked there.

EMILY:
Look again. He's sleeping in the corner.

MRS. HOLLINGER:
What a lot of rubbish.

ILSE:
No it isn't! She has the second sight! Believe me.

MRS. BRADSHAW:
I don't know what to do.

(A large and eccentric woman named MRS. McINTYRE steps out from the group that has been listening.)

MRS. McINTYRE:
I would do what the lassie says.

MRS. HOLLINGER:
What?

MRS. McINTYRE:
Go and look in the old Clifford place. I'll wager ye'll find the bairn waiting just like she said.

ILSE:
Emily, are you all right?

MRS. McINTYRE:
She can stay with me. Go. *(The others leave. She crosses to EMILY.)* The second sight. Will ye no have Highlandmen for your forefathers?

Emily:
Yes.

Mrs. McIntyre:
I should have guessed . . . we're very much alike, we two. Ach, dinna look at me like that, Emily. I am no common person. I am the woman who spanked the king.

Emily:
Excuse me?

Mrs. McIntyre:
Ach aye, I spanked the king. Of course, he would not be the king then, he was no but a wee prince. It was a long time ago, before ever we left the Old Country, and we lived near the Balmoral Castle. You might remember that Queen Victoria and Prince Albert would travel up to Balmoral every summer and bringing their children with them. *(Some of the listening ENSEMBLE use hats, scarves, etc. to turn themselves into Albert, Victoria, etc .)* and when they needed some more help at the Castle, they just sent for me. Listen to me, dear, and I'll tell you all about it . . .

They say Prince Bertie was a daring lad,

Albert:
the spittin' image of his royal dad.

Victoria:
But then one day
he went astray . . .

Albert, Victoria and Friends:

And Mistress Meg got mighty mad.

Mrs. McIntyre:

I told him not to!

Albert, Victoria and Friends:

When he came back she bopped his
royal bum
until it made the Highlands ring.

Albert:

You won't believe it, friend, but there she is.

All:

Mistress Meg, the Woman who spanked
the king.

Emily:

Mrs. McIntyre, will you let me write that story down, and publish it?

Mrs. McIntyre:

Will you be meaning that it will be printed in a paper?

Emily:

Or a magazine. I shall write it exactly as you told it. I could not better it by a syllable!

Mrs. McIntyre:

I'm no but a poor ignorant body, but maybe you will be knowing best.

EMILY:
Just trust me.

MRS. MCINTYRE:
That I do, child, that I do.

EMILY:
This is what I
hoped for, prayed for

MRS. MCINTYRE:
A tale that you were
born for, made for.

EMILY:
Relax
and let her tell it true,

MRS. MCINTYRE:
You can tell it too
and that's all you've got to do.

EMILY:
Then later
I can shape it
slightly, lightly . . .

MRS. MCINTYRE:
and give it your own special zing.

EMILY:
I think I even have the perfect title:

BOTH:

how about . . .
"The Woman Who Spanked the King"?

(EMILY starts scribbling down notes as ILSE enters and goes to MRS. McINTYRE.)

ILSE:
They found the Bradshaw boy, exactly where she said!

MRS. MCINTYRE:
I knew they would.

ILSE:
It's just like her Cousin Jimmy said, "With what you see, you will save three people. The first your dearest friend, the next a total stranger . . . "

EMILY: *(spots ILSE and runs over, interrupting)*
Ilse, a wonderful thing has happened.

ILSE: *(with a look at MRS. McINTYRE)*
I know.

EMILY:
I have heard the most charming story, and I am going to write that story and send it to Janet Royal at *Roche's Magazine*.

ILSE:
Emily, be realistic . . . she's rejected all your other stories.

Emily:
But this is real! Not some made-up fairy tale. She will publish it! She'll have to!

Mrs. McIntyre:
But first you have to write it.,

Ilse:
And then you have to mail it.

Emily:
And then we have to wait.

Mrs. McIntyre: *(after a beat)*
Where is *Roche's Magazine*?

Emily:
It's in New York City.

Mrs. McIntyre:
New York City? We'll have to wait forever.

Emily:
Not once they read it!

(On the other side of the stage, a brisk, trimly tailored, attractive woman named JANET ROYAL enters, pursued by her EDITORS.)

Editor #1:
Miss Royal, Miss Royal!

Janet:
Can't you see I'm busy, Mr. Barlow?

EDITOR #2:
Miss Royal, we have just read the most amazing story . . .

EDITOR #3:
. . . and we know you're going to love it.

EDITOR #4:
It's written by a young woman named Emily Starr . . .

EDITOR #1:
. . . and she's from Prince Edward Island.

JANET:
But *I'm* from Prince Edward Island . . .

ALL FOUR EDITORS:
Exactly!

(They start passing pages of EMILY's story to her.)

JANET:
What is this? From PEI . . .

EDITOR #1:
So fresh,

EDITOR #2:
So fine.

JANET:
I'm loving every line.

Editors #3 and #4:
By gum, we've found a story

All Four Editors:
that will lead us all to glory.
Shout

Janet:
Hooray,

All Four Editors:
Hooray!

Janet and Editors:
Today we raise a glass and sing.
This tale she told
is fourteen-karat gold.
Everybody will love "The Woman Who Spanked the King."

Janet:
Now what shall we do with this marvelous miss?

Editors:
And her fabulous tale,

Janet:
Which is absolute bliss!

Editors:
We should write her at once.

JANET:

No, we'll send her a wire,
which is bound to impress, sure to inspire.
We'll tell her we'll publish her tale right away.

EDITORS:

That's an absolute lie, cause we're booked
till May!

JANET:

But we have to make room for a talent
like hers,
she'll be decked out in diamonds, swaddled
in furs.
Bigger than all the Brontës combined.

EDITORS:

She's the kind of a writer we're dying to find!

JANET:

So we'd better make certain she won't
slip away.
Let's get the ball rolling . . .

JANET and EDITORS:

. . . and sign her today!

(The entire stage bursts into life, as a telegram travels from New York to Prince Edward Island, and then unites the whole town around EMILY.)

EDITOR #1:

Telegram for Emily Starr!

Messenger Boy:
Telegram for Emily Starr!

Dispatcher:
Telegram for Emily Starr!

Postman:
Telegram for Emily Starr!

Townspeople:
Telegram, telegram, telegram, telegram,
telegram for Miss Emily Starr!

Emily: *(bursting through the crowd.)*
Here I am, Miss Emily Starr!

Townspeople:
It's a telegram for you!
Don't go away! What does it say?
What does it say? What does it say?

Emily: *(reading, holding in her excitement)*
Miss Emily Starr, on behalf of *Roche's Magazine* . . .

Janet and Emily:
I am pleased to offer you $50 for the publication of your fine and original story . . .

Janet, Emily and Mrs. McIntyre: *(breaking through the crowd)*
"The Woman Who Spanked the King!"

(The three groups sing together in counterpoint as they march all around the stage in celebration.)

Mrs. McIntyre and Group 1:
They say Prince Bertie was a daring lad *etc.*

Emily and Group 2:
This is what I hoped for *etc.*

Janet and Group 3:
What is this? *etc.*

Mrs. McIntyre:
I spanked the kid!

Emily:
I'm glad you did!

All:
How we love the Woman who spanked
the King!

(TEDDY pulls EMILY from the crowd, reading the magazine, and leads her to the clearing in front of the Disappointed House.)

Teddy:
I am so proud of you, Emily! To read your own words in print . . .

Emily:
It's a small piece of rainbow gold.

Teddy:
But a true one.

EMILY:
And I found it right here at home.

TEDDY:
So you're wondering why I have to go so far away.

EMILY:
Teddy. I believe in you. No matter where you go, what you do. But you can't blame me for being sad that you're leaving.

TEDDY:
I'll be back. I'll whistle like I always did, and you'll know it's me. *(He whistles, but EMILY is still sad.)* It's the Tomorrow Road, Emily, calling both of us. The Yesterday Road and the Today Road are gone now . . . and they'll never come again.

EMILY:

There will be another autumn,
made of apricot and gold.
All the leaves in scarlet splendor
suddenly surrender,
running from the cold.
There will be another autumn,
blazing beauty everywhere.
But the emptiness of autumn
is that you will not be there.

TEDDY:

There will be another winter,
carved from ivory and pearl.
As the silver shadows hide you,

no one is beside you,
solitary girl.
There will be another winter,
white with wonder, like a bride.
But the loneliness of winter
is you won't be by my side.

Both:

Then in the springtime,
for there will be another springtime,
a mist of blossoms, a multi-colored haze.
We'll build a bower
for what will come tomorrow,
and weave a garland from all our yesterdays.

Emily:

There will be another summer,
set in amethyst and jade.

Teddy:

And the lilac light will find there
dreams we left behind there,
promises we made.

Both:

There will be a summer shower,
then the sky above will clear.

Emily:

There will be another rainbow.

Teddy:

We must wait another year.

Emily:

Do you see that star, Teddy? I want you to promise me that whenever you see it, you'll remember that I am thinking of you . . . and believing in you forever.

(They finally embrace and kiss, tentatively at first, and then passionately.)

Teddy:

We'll think of each other, always . . . as long as we live . . . .

Both:

There will be a sudden shower,
then the clouds will fly away . . .

Teddy:

We shall see another rainbow.

Emily:

Promise me another rainbow.

Both:

There will be another rainbow.
You and I will make it stay.

(The scene changes around them. It is November, over a year later. ELIZABETH is rolling out piecrust in the kitchen, and LAURA is at her needlepoint. JIMMY enters with the mail.)

Elizabeth:

Mind you don't go tracking snow into my clean kitchen, James Murray.

JIMMY:
God sends the snow from the sky to the ground, and some of it is bound to end up on my boots.

LAURA:
Amen to that.

ELIZABETH:
Was there any mail?

JIMMY:
Only for Emily.

(He holds out a large envelope.)

LAURA:
Thick or thin?

JIMMY:
Thick, I'm afraid.

LAURA:
Oh dear . . .

ELIZABETH:
I beg your pardon?

JIMMY:
I suspect it's the novel again.

ELIZABETH: *(not believing her ears)*
The novel? What novel?

LAURA:
The Tomorrow Road.

ELIZABETH:
Are you telling me that Emily has written a novel?

LAURA:
What do you think she was doing last winter? All those nights she'd stay up writing . . .

ELIZABETH:
I thought it was just more of her scribbling.

JIMMY:
Don't you call it scribbling, Elizabeth Murray! It's the best book I've ever read, and I've read it twenty times!

LAURA:
She only let us read it once before she sent it away.

JIMMY: *(crosses to his corner of the kitchen)*
I kept her handwritten copy, the one she thought she threw away after she finished making this fancy one on the typewriter. When I'm lonely, or scared, I take it out and read it again. It's like having Emily talk to me. That makes me happy for a while.

ELIZABETH:
The only book I read is the Holy Bible, and that makes me happy enough. I need no novels.

LAURA:
Emily needs it. She has to write.

ELIZABETH:
Nonsense. A body only has to do five things: eat, sleep, work, pray . . .

ALL THREE:
. . . and die.

JIMMY:
But Emily's different.

LAURA:
She can't just sit here, waiting for letters from Teddy Kent that never come.

ELIZABETH:
A painter of pictures. What kind of career is that for a man?

JIMMY:
A fine one, if you believe the newspapers.

LAURA:
Teddy Kent has become quite famous in London.

ELIZABETH:
Too famous, it would seem, for our Emily.

JIMMY:
I'm glad Dean Priest came by to visit her tonight.

ELIZABETH:
I suppose half a man is better than no man at all.

LAURA:
I know what Emily is feeling and my heart breaks for her.

ELIZABETH:
The tears of an old maid . . . what good are they?

(LAURA looks at her, decides not to speak, then exits.)

JIMMY:
You should read Emily's book, Elizabeth. It would help you understand her.

ELIZABETH:
And what do you understand of anything, James Murray?

JIMMY: *(after a pause)*
I suppose half a brain is better than no brain at all.

(JIMMY exits to his room. ELIZABETH stands motionless. She hears laughter from outside and quickly exits as EMILY and PRIEST enter.)

EMILY:
Oh, Dean, why did you have to move so far away?

PRIEST:
The school board commands and I must follow.

EMILY:

I'm the only one who stayed in Blair Water. It was dreadful this past year without you and Ilse and Perry . . . and Teddy.

PRIEST:

But surely they wrote to you.

EMILY:

A few chatty notes from Ilse and Perry. But nothing from Teddy. Nothing at all.

PERRY:

I thought Teddy Kent was very fond of you.

EMILY:

So did I. But no matter. I still have my writing to comfort me.

PRIEST:

We don't *all* forget you when we go away, Starr. I carry a picture of you in my mind wherever I go.

EMILY:

I'm sure you have better things to carry in your mind than a picture of me.

PRIEST:

Oh, Starr, I see you all the time, sitting up there in your room by that old lookout window, spinning your pretty cobwebs.

Emily:
Do you think what I write is nothing but cobwebs, Dean?

Priest:
Starr, I'm glad you can amuse yourself by writing. It's a splendid thing to have a little hobby . . .

Emily:
A little hobby? I've just realized that we've been together for hours, and you haven't mentioned my novel . . . although, perhaps, that is mention enough.

Priest:
I did read it, Starr. *(He stops.)*

Emily:
Dean, my book has been rejected by four . . . *(She notices the envelope JIMMY has brought in with him.)* . . . by *five* publishers. If you tell me there's any good in it, I'll keep on trying. Otherwise . . .

Priest: *(after a pause)*
It's a pretty little story. Pretty and flimsy and ephemeral as a rose-colored cloud. Cobwebs, nothing but cobwebs.

Emily:
You didn't talk like that when we first met, Dean. You used to think that I could do something someday.

PRIEST:
Forgive me, Starr, but you can't write about feelings that you've never really known.

EMILY:
You have no right to say that! You have no idea what feelings I keep locked inside me.

PRIEST:
Oh, I do, Starr, they're right here in these pages. *(He holds up the manuscript.)* Is this all you have to tell the world? Such a very little love. Such a very little book.

(PRIEST tosses the manuscript down and exits. EMILY takes the last copy of her manuscript, and climbs the stairs to her room. She kneels in front of the fireplace, and begins reading.)

EMILY:
"Do you see those three paths? I call the first one the Yesterday Road, because it used to be lovely, but it isn't any more." *(EMILY tears out the page .)* "And that one in the middle is the Today Road, because it is lovely right now." *(She keeps tearing out pages and throwing them into the fire with a calm intensity.)* "But that one over there may not look like much at the moment, but I promise you it *is* going to be lovely someday. That's the Tomorrow Road, my friends, and that's the road we're all on."

(The fire has grown dangerously, and smoke fills the room. EMILY struggles to make her way for the door.)

Help me, please! Somebody! Cousin Jimmy! Aunt Laura! Aunt Elizabeth!

(The smoke has blinded her, and she can't see where she's going. With a terrible scream, she falls down the stairs as the stage is plunged into darkness.

When the lights come up, it's six months later, a beautiful day in May. We're on the road to Blair Water. ELIZABETH encounters DR. BURNLEY.)

ELIZABETH:
Have you seen Emily?

DR. BURNLEY:
I have just examined her.

ELIZABETH:
What is wrong with her leg, Allan?

DR. BURNLEY:
Absolutely nothing. It's been six months since her fall. The bone has healed, there's no muscular damage.

ELIZABETH:
Then why must she still walk with a cane?

DR. BURNLEY:
Only Emily can tell you that. Good day to you. (*He exits.)*

ELIZABETH:
But Dr. Burnley . . . Allan . . . *(She starts after him, but is stopped by JIMMY and LAURA, trying to get past her in a great hurry.)* Where are you two going?

LAURA:
We've got some errands to run.

ELIZABETH:
I could have done them for you.

JIMMY:
I don't think so.

LAURA:
Not these errands.

JIMMY:
I've got to mail an important package.

ELIZABETH:
Nonsense! You don't *have* anything important . . .

JIMMY:
You'd be surprised, Elizabeth.

LAURA:
Come on, Jimmy, let's be on our way.

(LAURA and JIMMY exit. ELIZABETH is next stopped by the entrance of EMILY.)

ELIZABETH:
And where are you going, child? You shouldn't be walking.

EMILY:
I'm sure Dr. Burnley told you what he told me: that I'm perfectly fine, and the weakness is all in my mind.

ELIZABETH:
I don't pay heed to that kind of talk.

EMILY:
Fine. Then leave me to myself.

ELIZABETH:
But, child, you're too much by yourself. You won't see anyone. You won't write to anyone . . . and Teddy Kent has sent you three letters since the accident.

EMILY:
But what do I have to tell him? That I can't write? That I can't walk? Do you think that's the kind of message the famous and successful Mr. Kent wants to hear? *(Starts to leave.)*

ELIZABETH:
Emily, where are you going?

EMILY:
I'm meeting Dean.

Elizabeth:
Old Jarback Priest? But you haven't seen him since . . .

Emily:
. . . since the night I fell. But he wants to meet me to ask a particular question. Oh, I know what he's going to ask, Aunt Elizabeth, and I know what my answer must be.

Elizabeth:
No girl, don't! You'll find a better match than Priest!

Emily:
Who, Aunt Elizabeth? Tell me his name. No young men come up the road to our door any more. Those days are gone.

Elizabeth:
The man is a lonely cripple.

Emily:
And am I that much different? It's just as God said to Noah "Take two of every sort, according to their kind."

(ELIZABETH exits, as EMILY stands still and the set changes to the Disappointed House.)

Priest:
I hoped you would come.

EMILY:
And why wouldn't I?

PRIEST:
Because your accident was my fault.

EMILY:
Did you tear my novel apart and burn it?

PRIEST:
But I told you it was worthless.

EMILY:
No, Dean, you only showed me how foolish all my dreams had been. Emily the poet, climber of the Alpine Path, pursuer of the rainbow gold. That life is over now.

PRIEST:
Then let a new life begin with me . . . I can make you happy. I know I can, Starr. That's what you've always seemed to me: an exquisite star, just out of my reach.

TEDDY: *(appearing in a vision)*
We'll think of each other always . . . as long as we live . . .

EMILY: *(to the vision of TEDDY)*
No.

PRIEST:
Yes, Starr, that's why I bought us this house.

Emily:
The Disappointed House?

Priest:
I recognized it from the way you wrote about it. I could tell how much it meant to you, and I wanted us to share it . . .

Disappointed house,
let the love begin.
Throw the shutters wide,
show the sunlight in.

Teddy and Priest:
We have found the key,
open up the door.
For the disappointed house . . .

Teddy:
For the disappointed house
won't be disappointed any more.

Emily:
No, Dean, I can't. It was wrong of me to think that I ever could.

Priest:
It's still Teddy Kent, isn't it?

Emily:
Forgive me, Dean.

PRIEST:
What is there to forgive? I can't help loving you, and you can't help loving him.

EMILY:
I don't know if I can love anyone, not anymore.

PRIEST:
I suppose in the end, it's only fair . . . I would have won you by a lie. That is why I could never keep you.

EMILY:
A lie?

PRIEST:
You asked me to tell the truth about your novel. I didn't. It was a good piece of work. Very good.

EMILY:
Why did you lie to me?

PRIEST:
Because you would have kept trying until you were successful, and then you would have been lost to me forever. Like you are now . . . And this still will be the Disappointed House . . . Goodbye, Starr.

(PRIEST exits.

EMILY has reached the centre of town when she hears a horn beep, a screech of brakes and a crash.)

PERRY: *(offstage)*
Why don't you watch where you're going, friend?

EMILY:
Perry? Perry Miller?

(PERRY enters, dressed as the big-city slicker, complete with auto goggles, etc., holding his steering wheel.)

PERRY:
Emily Starr! I've been looking everywhere for you.

EMILY:
Is that horseless carriage yours?

PERRY:
Yes, it's all mine . . . *(He looks at the wheel.)* . . . what's left of it. But we call them automobiles back on the mainland, Emily, and yes, it's all mine, bought with the fruits of my highly successful labors. Perry Miller, Q.C., and rising star in the political firmament.

EMILY:
Are you still going to be prime minister?

PERRY:
Indeed I am. You remember that conversation? I also said I was going to marry you.

EMILY:
I've tried to forget that part.

PERRY:

No more Stovepipe Town anymore. I've got the world by the tail now. Why can't you make up your mind to have me, Emily?

EMILY:

Listen, Perry, I like you. I'll always like you. But if you ever ask me to marry you again, I'll never speak to you as long as I live.

PERRY:

All right, then, that's enough about my problems. Now what about yours?

EMILY:

I don't have any problems.

PERRY:

Oh really? I guess you're still walking with a cane because you fancy the way it looks.

EMILY:

Why don't you speak your mind, Perry Miller?

PERRY:

Why don't you speak yours, Emily Starr? *(She does not answer.)* I haven't seen any of your stories in the magazines lately.

EMILY:

That's because I haven't written any. I took all of last year to write a novel, but not one publisher believed in it at all.

PERRY:
Do you still believe in it?

EMILY:
That doesn't matter.

PERRY:
Oh yes it does! That matters most of all . . . Listen to me, Emily . . . the first fancy party I was ever invited to in Ottawa was nearly the last . . . You see, I had brand new evening clothes, from the top hat right down to the very slippery shoes. And when they announced me, I started up the stairs, fell, and landed right where it hurts the most. It was that moment, Emily, that I had to make a choice. I could pick myself up, climb those stairs, and enter the world I'd always dreamed of, or else . . .

One step down
I'll be headin' to
Stovepipe Town,
where the future is
bleak and brown
all grimy and grey.

So dull and flat,
kid, when everything
feels like that,
it's the moment to
grab your hat
and be on your way.

Eyes on the top,
just start ascending.

Don't ever stop
till there's a happy ending,
no pretending.

Take it slow,
cause it isn't how
fast you go.
Here's a lesson you
need to know
before you can climb:
you can only go just one step
at a time.

One step back
I'll wind up in a
one-room shack
where tomorrow's so
cold and black
I feel I could cry.

Just let me say,
kid, when everything
looks that way,
it's the moment to
seize the day,
gotta learn to fly.

Don't ever doubt
what you've been chancing,
You'll figure out
that life's a lot like dancing:
keep advancing.

Take it slow,
cause it isn't how

fast you go.
Here's a lesson you
need to know
before you can climb:
you can only go just one step
at a time.

(The TOWNSPEOPLE back PERRY up in his message.)

MEN:
You'll learn that life will give you the lift
you need.

WOMEN:
It really will!

MEN
The only thing to do is pursue your lead,
and . . .

WOMEN:
One day you'll wake to find that you have
it all.

MEN:
You really do!

ALL: *(except PERRY)*
Take our tip if you trip,
never fall, have a ball!

(PERRY leads EMILY into a dance, where she discards her cane.)

ALL:

Take it slow . . .

PERRY:

Cause it isn't how . . .

ALL:

Fast you go.

PERRY:

Here's a lesson you
need to know . . .

ALL:

Before you can climb, climb, climb.

PERRY:

If you want to be Number One,
take a look at the way it's done.

ALL:

You can only go just one step . . .

PERRY:

At a time!

ALL:

Just one step, one step at a time!

(PERRY and EMILY vanish into the crowd. We are in the post office. LAURA is speaking to the POSTMISTRESS.)

LAURA:
Well, if there *are* any letters from New York, will you let me know right away?

POSTMISTRESS:
I will, Miss Murray.

(DR. BURNLEY enters.)

DR. BURNLEY:
Good day, Laura.

LAURA:
Good day, Allan.

DR. BURNLEY:
I haven't seen much of you in town.

LAURA:
I come in when I have something to do . . .

DR. BURNLEY:
. . . and you stay away when you don't.

LAURA:
I suppose.

DR. BURNLEY:
Do you think it's better that way?

LAURA:
Yes I do, Allan. Don't you?

Dr. Burnley: *(after a pause)*
And how is Emily?

(Before LAURA can answer, EMILY strides into the store without her cane.)

Emily:
I'd like a ream of writing paper, please. *(She sees the others.)* Excuse me, Aunt Laura, Dr. Burnley.

Dr. Burnley:
Emily! I'm so happy to see you walking again!

Emily:
Does it please you to know that you were right?

Dr. Burnley:
No, it pleases me to know you are well . . . and Ilse will be delighted.

Emily:
I'll write her.

(ILSE appears, a totally transformed creature. She is now the "woman of the theater," with a flamboyant wardrobe to match.)

Ilse:
Why don't you just tell me?

Emily:
Ilse, you didn't let me know you were coming.

ILSE:
I wanted to surprise you.

EMILY:
And you did!

ILSE: *(grandly)*
Father, don't you have any bones to set or babies to deliver? Anything that would let two beloved old friends renew their acquaintance in solitude?

DR. BURNLEY: *(exiting)*
Daughter, I don't practise medicine all the time. Must you be acting all the time?

(ILSE takes EMILY's arm and they wander away from town.)

ILSE:
So, where shall we go? The beach? The forest? The tomorrow road?

EMILY:
My leg is still rather weak, Ilse . . . maybe we could rest here for a while.

ILSE:
If it makes you happy, dearest friend.

EMILY:
Perry Miller came to see me the last time he was in town.

Ilse:
And of course he threw himself at your feet, and you rejected him with scorn. You ice-cold creature, have you ever really loved anything except that pen of yours?

Emily:
Ilse, I know you always cared for Perry . . .

Ilse:
. . . and you never understood, did you, Emily? And so you thought me an idiot. Maybe I was, but I've changed. And I've decided that when a girl can't get the thing she really wants, she can't help chasing after something else.

Emily: *(a horrible suspicion dawning)*
What do you mean?

Ilse:
Emily, darling, wish me luck . . . I'm going to marry Teddy Kent.

Emily:
Oh, Ilse . . . *(She keeps her composure.)* . . . I'm so very happy . . . for both of you.

Ilse:
I know he used to be sweet on you, but that was years ago. And then, after your accident, when you didn't answer any of his letters, he thought you'd given up on him forever. I guess it was only natural that the two of us, so far away from home, should become close. Well, I finally told him I couldn't do

without him, and he said I'd either have to do without him or marry him. And so here we are . . .

(ILSE keeps talking, as the GIRLS from EMILY's school days reappear, now grown and dressed as brides, to haunt her still. JENNIE STRANG leads them once again.)

GIRLS:

The Murrays are an old lot,
they came here years ago.
The Murrays are a cold lot,
there isn't much they show.
The Murrays take their feelings
and lock them up inside.

Then they throw away the key,
and the only thing you see
is the Murray pride,
the Murray pride,
the Murray pride . . .

ILSE:

Besides, Teddy is going to be very famous. Won't it be wonderful to be the wife of a famous man?

EMILY:

If that's what you want, Ilse.

JENNIE STRANG:

Why are you so vain and haughty?
What gives you that lofty air?
Acting like the Queen of Sheba,
when you're just a prickly pear.

Dressed up like your old Aunt Laura,
puffed up like a popinjay.
You'll be getting your comeuppance:
Ilse Burnley's Wedding Day!

GIRLS:

We know the Bible tells us
about the sin of Pride.
Worst of the Seven Deadly,
the evil you can't hide.
And so prepare, you sinner,
to hear that trumpet call.
Because it's pride, pride, pride, pride, pride
that goes before the fall.

ILSE:

Oh, Emily, I must be the luckiest girl in all the world!

EMILY:

In all the world? Surely in all the universe.

JENNIE:

Why are you so self-important?
Who made you the Holy Grail?

GIRLS:

Not a man was ever worthy,
every one was bound to fail.

JENNIE:

Isn't she just like a Murray?
Never cares for anything.

Girls:

Maybe we'll see some emotion,
when she hears that church bell ring.

We know the Bible tells us
about the sin of Pride.
Worst of the Seven Deadly,
the evil you can't hide.
And so prepare, you sinner,
to hear that trumpet call.
Because it's pride, pride, pride, pride . . .

Ilse:

And Emily . . .

Emily:

Yes, Ilse?

Ilse:

Of course, you'll be my bridesmaid?

Emily:

I would love to.

(EMILY dashes out of the house, the GIRLS pursuing her.)

Girls:

That goes before the fall.

(The GIRLS exit, laughing maniacally. EMILY crosses to the old tree where she first met PERRY. He is waiting there.)

PERRY:
At least you're the bridesmaid, Emily Starr . . . I guess Teddy thought he was too high and mighty to have Stovepipe Town as his best man.

EMILY:
You goose! It wasn't Teddy at all, it was Ilse.

PERRY:
Ilse?

EMILY:
Do you think she'd have you as the best man when she hoped for years you would be the groom?

PERRY:
She never thought of me that way . . . She always was nagging me about something. I could never please her.

EMILY:
Perry, if she hadn't liked you, do you suppose she would have cared what grammar you used, or what etiquette you smashed?

PERRY:
I suppose not.

EMILY:
All those years, and you never knew . . .

PERRY:
I know now.

EMILY:
But it's too late.

PERRY:
Is it ever too late to tell someone you love them?

(TEDDY appears, unseen by them.)

EMILY:
We pass through doors, Perry. Then we have to lock them tight, and throw away the key.

PERRY:
I've been a fool, Emily . . . and I would have been twice the fool for thinking that Teddy wasn't still my friend.

TEDDY:
He always will be, Perry. I hope you know that.

PERRY:
I know it now. Thanks to Emily. *(The three look at each other for an embarrassed moment. PERRY extends his hand to TEDDY.)* The best of luck to you and Ilse.

TEDDY: *(shaking his hand)*
Thank you, Perry.

PERRY:
Well . . . like they say, I'll see you in church. *(PERRY exits.)*

TEDDY:

You look well.

EMILY:

Do I, now?

TEDDY:

How's your leg?

EMILY:

As good as new. How's yours?

TEDDY:

Please, Emily, don't act this way.

EMILY:

What way? Isn't this the way you're supposed to act with a boy who promises to think of you forever and then vanishes off the face of the Earth?

TEDDY:

I didn't vanish off the face of the Earth.

EMILY:

You might as well have. Sixteen months without a word. Why, Teddy?

TEDDY:

Remember your dream? Both of us in search of rainbow gold? You told me I was going to be "the finest artist the world had ever seen." Well, maybe I could've been, Emily, but I never found out. You see, I gave up on the rainbow and just settled for the gold.

EMILY:
Isn't that what growing up means? Learning what you'll settle for?

TEDDY:
Don't talk like that! You sound like everyone else . . .

EMILY:
Maybe I am like everyone else.

TEDDY:
No, you're not! You're special . . .

EMILY:
And if I'm so special, why are you marrying Ilse?

TEDDY:
Because she needs me.

EMILY:
And I don't?

TEDDY:
You never really needed anyone, Emily.

EMILY: *(after a beat)*
I hope you and Ilse are very happy.

TEDDY:
Thank you.

EMILY:
Well, as Perry said, I'll see you in church.

TEDDY:
I suppose you will. Goodnight, Emily.

EMILY:
Goodbye, Teddy. *(He exits.)*

You'll sit painting,
and I'll write the whole day through.
You and me
sipping tea
while our dreams are coming . . .

(We hear an ear-splitting scream. It is ILSE in her wedding gown, tearing a bouquet of flowers apart.)

ILSE:
I won't let him ruin this day, I won't! I won't!

EMILY:
Who? Who sent you this?

ILSE:
Read his confounded card. *(ILSE stops tearing long enough to hand it to EMILY.)*

EMILY: *(reading)*
"To Ilse, with the best wishes of her old friend, Perry."

ILSE:
Not today, Perry Miller! Not today!

EMILY:
Ilse, have you gone crazy?

ILSE: *(ripping petals off the last flower)*
I love him not, I love him not, I love him not! There! I can go through with it now.

(DR. BURNLEY appears at the door.)

DR. BURNLEY:
We'd best be going, Ilse. Teddy's at the church already.

(A NEIGHBOUR rushes on.)

NEIGHBOUR:
Dr. Burnley, you have to come at once!

DR. BURNLEY:
What is it?

NEIGHBOUR:
It's Perry Miller! He crashed his car on the way to the church.

ILSE:
Is he still alive?

NEIGHBOUR:
I think so. Hurry, Dr. Burnley!

ILSE:
Perry, oh Perry! I'm coming . . . !

(DR. BURNLEY follows off, chasing after ILSE, pursued by the NEIGHBOURS. Only EMILY and her family are left.)

JIMMY:
My, my, what a day.

ELIZABETH:
What a disgrace! What a scandal!

LAURA:
But if Ilse really loved Perry Miller . . .

ELIZABETH:
. . . then why did she promise to marry Teddy Kent? Can you tell me that?

EMILY:
"When a girl can't get the thing she wants, she can't help chasing after something else."

(They all leave. EMILY bends down to pick up the flowers. She doesn't notice JANET ROYAL come to the door, and stand there watching her.)

JANET:
When I read someone's writing, I try to guess what they look like. I'm usually wrong. But not this time.

EMILY:
Pardon me?

JANET:
If you asked me to describe Emily Starr, I would have said she looks . . . just like you.

EMILY:
I'm afraid I haven't had the pleasure of your acquaintance.

JANET:
How rude of me! Of course. *(Extends her hand.)* Emily, I'm Janet Royal.

EMILY:
Miss Royal! This is an honor!

JANET:
The honor is mine. To meet the author of so many of our successful stories . . . and our first novel.

EMILY: *(stopping dead)*
I beg your pardon?

JANET:
I've been thinking of expanding our publishing operations, and the arrival of your book seemed the sign that we should do it. *The Tomorrow Road* . What a prophetic title!

EMILY:
The Tomorrow Road? Excuse me, Miss Royal, but I must sit down. *(And she does.)*

JANET:
Emily, what's wrong?

EMILY:
Miss Royal, I never sent you *The Tomorrow Road*.

JANET:
I know, but your Cousin Jimmy did. It was a bit of a struggle to read that handwritten manuscript, but I felt it would be worth the effort.

EMILY:
Cousin Jimmy . . .

JANET: *(taking some documents from her valise)*
I've brought the contracts for your signature. I'm sure you'll find the terms more than equitable.

EMILY:
I'm sure.

JANET:
But I didn't travel all the way back home to the Island to get a contract signed.

EMILY:
Then why have you come?

JANET:
Emily, I want you to come back to New York with me. You mustn't waste your life here. It was just the place for you to grow up. But now you must move on, to the center of things. If you do, I promise that Emily Starr will be a name to conjure with.

EMILY:
But to leave this place I love, and these people I love . . .

JANET:
I was just like you once, Emily, but I made my choice. I had to leave, and so do you . . .

EMILY:
No, Miss Royal. Thank you, but I can't.

JANET:
Don't do this to yourself, Emily.

EMILY:
I may not succeed here, Miss Royal, but if not, then I wouldn't succeed in New York, either. All I know is that some fountain of living water would dry up in my soul if I left the land I love.

JANET:
You can sign down there.

EMILY:
I'm not going, Miss Royal.

JANET:
I know. But I'll publish your book, anyway. Emily Starr . . . all the good wishes ever thought, said or written, go with you. *(She exits.)*

EMILY:

Why do I love this island?
Why do I love this land?
There's something in its beauty
that I understand.

The copper of its beaches,
and the silver of its shore.
It is these,
and so much more.

I know I love this island,
this place that stands apart.
I welcome every morning
as it fills my heart.

I know I love its people,
and I know that they are strong,
and I know
that I belong.

I believe the hand of God will guide me
as I live between the sea and sky.
And I pray my children stand beside me
for it's here I'll stay until I die.

(EMILY is surrounded by the TOWNSPEOPLE.)

Yes, I pray my children stand beside me
for it's here I'll stay until I die.

(The music changes to an urgent tone. The TOWNSPEOPLE transform into an eager crowd. EMILY stands reading a letter.)

PURSER:
All ashore that's going ashore! All ashore that's going ashore!

(TEDDY appears in a pool of light.)

Teddy:
Dear Emily, why did I run back to England as soon as I could? I don't know. All I *do* know is that I'm running again. This time to New York. I sail today, on the fastest and grandest ship ever built.

Emily:
Teddy . . .

Purser:
Last call for those going ashore!

Teddy:
Goodbye for now, Emily.

Emily: *(a scream)*
Teddy, no!

(Everything suddenly freezes.)

Teddy:
I hear your voice,
I hear it call me.
I hear it call through the wind and the foam.
I hear it still,
I hear it call me:
"Hurry now, hurry home . . ."

Jimmy's Voice:
With what you see, you will save three people: the first, your dearest friend, the next, a total stranger . . .

Teddy:
. . . and the last your own true love.

Emily:
Run, Teddy, run!

Teddy:
Get me off this ship.

Purser:
But they're raising the gangplank.

Teddy:
Then lower it. I've got to get off.

Purser:
There are hundreds of people who'd give anything to be in your place.

Teddy:
Then they can have my ticket. Here!

(TEDDY throws the ticket to the crowd who swirl around him, and the scene vanishes. Out of the darkness, a bunch of candles appear. We are back in the kitchen at New Moon, and LAURA, JIMMY and ELIZABETH bring out a birthday cake for EMILY.)

Jimmy:
There's the birthday girl!

Laura:
Blow them all out with one breath and you get your wish.

Elizabeth:
That's nonsense, Laura . . . but take a deep breath anyway.

LAURA:
And here's a special letter for you.

EMILY: *(excitedly)*
From London?

ELIZABETH: *(gently)*
No, child, it's not from London.

JIMMY:
It's from you.

LAURA:
It's the letter you wrote to yourself on your fourteenth birthday . . . to be opened ten years later.

EMILY: *(opens the letter and slowly reads it aloud)*
"Oh, Twenty-Four, it must be splendid to be you! Have you written your great book? Have you climbed to the very top of the Alpine Path? Are you a staid old married woman now, with several children, living with . . . *(She stops reading, and skips ahead.)* . . . I hope you are happy and famous and lovely, and that you haven't quite forgotten . . . Emily, at Fourteen."

JIMMY: *(breaking the silence)*
I think it's a lovely letter.

EMILY:
So now I see the pattern of my life. Year after year the seasons will walk by my door. I will know the beauty of nature, and the comfort of my writing. That will be all, and that will be enough.

LAURA:
But what if someone . . .

EMILY:
There will be no someone. Let me hear no more of that.

LAURA:
Don't say that, please!

EMILY:
Let me hear no more of that.

(She exits.)

LAURA:
Emily . . .

ELIZABETH:
Let her go, Laura . . . we have to let her go.

LAURA: *(to ELIZABETH)*
And did you hear our father's voice just then?

ELIZABETH:
No, Laura. I heard my own.

LAURA:

Start by breathing in now,
warm and deep and slow.
That's how you begin now,
then you let it go.
Time for letting go.

JIMMY:

Children are like flowers:
love them and they grow.
Years fly by in hours,
and before you know,
time for letting go.

LAURA and JIMMY:

Letting go
may seem the wisest thing to do,
even so,
when it is happening to you,
you pretend
that you're not really holding on.
In the end,
you wake up and find they've gone,
gone away.
They never stay.

ELIZABETH:

Feelings you can't measure,
love you can't explain.
Sweetest sort of pleasure,
purest kind of pain.

ELIZABETH, LAURA and JIMMY:

Let it go again . . .
See the seasons changing,
getting set to snow.
Time for rearranging,
time for letting go.

LAURA:

Love is letting go.

JIMMY:
Life is letting go.

ELIZABETH:
Time for letting go.

(The FAMILY embrace and exit. We see EMILY waiting alone outside the Disappointed House.)

EMILY:
There will be another winter,
carved from ivory and pearl.
As the silver shadows hide you,
no one is beside you,
solitary girl.
There will be another winter,
white with wonder, like a bride.
But the loneliness of winter
is you won't . . .

(She can't finish, and dissolves in tears. Then she hears TEDDY's whistle, and his voice.)

TEDDY: *(offstage)*
Then in the springtime,
for there will be another springtime.

EMILY: *(still not believing)*
A mist of blossoms,
a multi-colored haze.

(TEDDY appears. EMILY sees him, and they rush into an embrace as the music swells around them.)

TEDDY:
We shall see another rainbow.

EMILY:
Promise me another rainbow.

BOTH:
There will be another rainbow.
You and I will make it stay.

(We gradually transform into a wedding ceremony. ILSE and PERRY appear.)

ILSE:
Oh, Perry, look at her! She's such a beautiful bride.

PERRY:
And so are you, Mrs. Miller. I've learned something, you know.

ILSE:
And what would that be, Mr. Miller?

PERRY:
Once a fella stops chasing after something else . . .

ILSE:
. . . he gets the thing he really wants.

(We see LAURA, ELIZABETH and JIMMY.)

LAURA:
I still think she has her mother's smile.

Jimmy:
And I see her father's eyes. What about you, Elizabeth?

Elizabeth:
I think she looks like Emily . . . and that's a wonderful thing to be.

Emily:
I see a star,
I see it shine now
I see it shine through the night,
to the day.
It lights the path
that will be mine now,
come what might,
come what may . . .

I was born
to tell this story.
This is how,
this is when
this is where the dream begins!

(EMILY looks towards the future, surrounded by the love of her family and friends, as the curtain falls.)

(End of ACT II)

FOUR SONGS

SELECTIONS FROM THE MUSICAL

"EMILY"

... based on "EMILY OF NEW MOON", "EMILY CLIMBS" and "EMILY'S QUEST" by Lucy Maud Montgomery.

BOOK AND LYRICS: RICHARD OUZOUNIAN

MUSIC: MAREK NORMAN

1. THE DREAM BEGINS
2. DISAPPOINTED HOUSE
3. THERE WILL BE ANOTHER RAINBOW
4. THIS ISLAND

THE DREAM BEGINS

[from the musical, "EMILY"]

LYRICS: RICHARD OUZOUNIAN

MUSIC: MAREK NORMAN

11 Poco Piu Mosso
COME WHAT MIGHT, COME WHAT MAY.
I SEE THE SKY SO DARK AND STEA-DY.
poco piu mosso...
poco cresc.
cresc.
I SEE THE MOON, HOW IT GRINS.
THE HEA-VENS SMILE AND I AM REA-DY. FOR
cresc. poco a poco...
cresc.
sost.
rall. (et dim.)
*RIT'EN. (calando...)
THIS IS WHERE THE DREAM BE- GINS.
rall. (et dim.)

05/03/00-MN

(piano/vocal) THE DREAM BEGINS (from the musical, "EMILY")

LYRICS: RICHARD OUZOUNIAN MUSIC: MAREK NORMAN

DISAPPOINTED HOUSE

from the musical, "EMILY"

LYRICS: RICHARD OUZOUNIAN

MUSIC: MAREK NORMAN

DISAPPOINTED HOUSE cont.
p. 2
a tempo...
un poco acce.
12 PIU MOSSO (poco)
ALL THE DOORS ARE LOCKED,
NO ONE HAS THE
KEY.
NO ONE CLIMBS THE STAIR,
un poco acce.
cresc.
PIU MOSSO (poco)
cresc.
un poco rall.
RITEN. et dim.
a tempo...
NO ONE DIMS THE LIGHT.
WHEN IT'S DARK AND COLD,
NO ONE HOLDS YOU TIGHT.
DREAM-ING OF A LOVE
dim. et rall.
20 ALLEGRO AMABILE
IT HAS NE-VER KNOWN.
DIS-AP-POIN-TED HOUSE,
SIT-TING ALL A-
LONE.
BUT IM-

p.3 DISAPPOINTED HOUSE cont.

DISAPPOINTED HOUSE cont. p.4
Cresc.
36 APPASSIONATA!
UP TO FIND — A FRIEND. WE'LL A- WA-KEN TO THE MORN-ING GOD—
Cresc.
(...like Church bells)
HAS MADE. TOAST AND BA-CON, AND A POT OF
(GRAND ALLARGANDO!)
44 MENO MOSSO... (CALANDO)
MAR-MA-LADE. I'LL SIT PAINT-ING, AND YOU'LL WRITE THE WHOLE — DAY

p. 5 DISAPPOINTED HOUSE cont.
dim. et rall. (poco a poco...)
Slowly... and gently
THROUGH. YOU AND ME, SIP-PING TEA, WHILE OUR DREAMS ARE CO-MING...
dim. et rall. (poco a poco)
51 TEMPO PRIMA (♩=92 m.m.)
TRUE.
55 MOLTO DELICATO
ALLARGANDO...
DIS-AP-POIN-TED HOUSE, LET THE LOVE BE-GIN. THROW THE SHUT-TERS WIDE, SHOW THE SUN-LIGHT IN.
cresc. poco a poco...
ALLARGANDO...

04/26/00-MN

(piano/vocal) DISAPPOINTED HOUSE (from the musical, "EMILY")

LYRICS: RICHARD OUZOUNIAN

MUSIC: MAREK NORMAN

THERE WILL BE ANOTHER RAINBOW

[from the musical, "EMILY"]

LYRICS: RICHARD OUZOUNIAN MUSIC: MAREK NORMAN

un poco cresc
dim
9.
10.
11.
12.
mf
(1. SPLEN-DOR SUD-DEN-LY SUR-REN-DER, RUN-NING FROM THE COLD.
THERE WILL BE A-NO-THER
(2. HIDE YOU, NO ONE IS BE-SIDE YOU, SO-LI-TAR-Y GIRL.
THERE WILL BE A-NO-THER
13.
14.
15.
16.
(1. AU-TUMN,
BLA-ZING BEAU-TY EV-'RY-WHERE.
BUT THE EMP-TI-NESS OF
(2. WIN-TER,
WHITE WITH WON-DER, LIKE A BRIDE.
BUT THE LONE-LI-NESS OF

1ST
SOLO MAN:
(1. AU-TUMN
IS THAT YOU WILL NOT BE
THERE.
(2. THERE WILL BE A-NO-THER
(2. WIN-TER
IS YOU WON'T BE BY MY... (to 2ND end.)
delicato...
2ND
BOTH:
(gently)
23
ARIOSO...
... SIDE.
THEN IN THE
SPRING-TIME,
FOR THERE WILL BE A-NO-THER
SPRING-TIME,
cresc.

cresc. poco a poco...
(poco allargando...
dim.
cresc.
DIV.
A MIST OF BLOS-SOMS, A MUL-TI-CO-LORED HAZE. WE'LL BUILD A
cresc. poco a poco...
(poco allargando...
31 APPASSIONATO...
(morendo...
WOMAN
BOW-ER FOR WHAT WILL COME TO-MOR ROW, AND WEAVE A
MAN
BOW-ER FOR WHAT WILL COME TO-MOR ROW, AND WEAVE A
(morendo...
sost.
BOTH
GAR-LAND FROM ALL OUR YES-TER-DAYS.
dim.

p. 5 THERE WILL BE ANOTHER RAINBOW cont.

52. WOMAN:
THERE WILL BE A-NO-THER RAIN - BOW.
53.
54.
55.
MAN: *riten.
WE MUST WAIT
56.
A-NO-THER
dim.
molto sostenuto ...
57 A TEMPO ... (poco rubato)
dim.
58.
59.
60.
un poco dim. et rall.
BOTH:
YEAR.
THERE WILL BE A SUD-DEN
61 AFFETUOSO ... (tempo prima)
62.
63.
64.
un poco ritard.
MAN:
BOTH
SHOW-ER,
THEN THE CLOUDS WILL FLY A-WAY ...
WE SHALL SEE A-NO-THER

A TEMPO (♩=60 m.m.)
(WOMAN)
PRO-MISE ME A-NO-THER RAIN- BOW...
THERE WILL BE A-NO-THER
RAIN - BOW ...
THERE WILL BE A-NO-THER
un poco rall.
cresc.
dim.
VERY SLOW...
(molto espressivo)
RAIN - BOW.
YOU AND I
WILL MAKE IT...
RAIN - BOW.
YOU AND I
WILL MAKE IT...
un poco rall.
VERY SLOW...
molto sostenuto...

05/02/00 - MN

(piano / vocal) **THERE WILL BE ANOTHER RAINBOW** (from the musical, "EMILY")

LYRICS: RICHARD OUZOUNIAN

MUSIC: MAREK NORMAN

This Island

[from the musical, "EMILY"]

Lyrics: Richard Ouzounian

Music: Marek Norman

A TEMPO...
11
(dim. et rall.)
cresc. poco a poco...
THESE, AND SO MUCH MORE. I KNOW I LOVE THIS IS-LAND, THIS PLACE THAT STANDS A-PART. I
(dim. et rall.)
A TEMPO... cresc. poco a poco...
...cresc. poco a poco...
WEL-COME EV'RY MORN-ING AS IT FILLS MY HEART. I KNOW I LOVE ITS PEO-PLE, AND I
...cresc. poco a poco...
(un poco allargando...
KNOW THAT THEY ARE STRONG, AND I KNOW THAT I BE - LONG. I BE-
(+8 basso...

p. 3 THIS ISLAND cont.

(piano/vocal) **THIS ISLAND** (from the musical, "EMILY")

LYRICS: RICHARD OUZOUNIAN — MUSIC: MAREK NORMAN